# Thinkers Against Modernity

## by

## Keith Preston

Thinkers Against Modernity

by

Keith Preston

Copyright © 2016
Black House Publishing Ltd

ISBN-13: 978-1-910881-23-1

This edition printed by
Amazon CreateSpace
for sale and distribution by
Amazon.com, Inc. and its affiliates.

Black House Publishing Ltd
Kemp House
152 City Road
London
United Kingdom
EC1V 2NX

www.blackhousepublishing.com
Email: info@blackhousepublishing.com

# Contents

Ernst Junger     1

Carl Schmitt     21

Friedrich Nietzsche     39

Hilaire Belloc     61

G. K. Chesterton     67

Julius Evola     75

Aleister Crowley     87

Corneliu Codreanu     101

Alain De Benoist     109

Bibliography     121

C. s. Lewis — 70

Enequality — 93

JP 2 - 1

# *Ernst Junger*

## Ernst Junger: The Resolute Life of an Anarch

Perhaps the most interesting, poignant and, possibly, threatening type of writer and thinker is the one who not only defies conventional categorizations of thought but also offers a deeply penetrating critique of those illusions many hold to be the most sacred. Ernst Junger (1895-1998), who first came to literary prominence during Germany's Weimar era as a diarist of the experiences of a front line storm trooper during the Great War, is one such writer. Both the controversial nature of his writing and its staying power are demonstrated by the fact that he remains one of the most important yet widely disliked literary and cultural figures of twentieth century Germany. As recently as 1993, when Junger would have been ninety-eight years of age, he was the subject of an intensely hostile exchange in the "New York Review of Books" between an admirer and a detractor of his work.[1] On the occasion of his one hundredth birthday in 1995, Junger was the subject of a scathing, derisive musical performed in East Berlin. Yet Junger was also the recipient of Germany's most prestigious literary awards, the Goethe Prize and the Schiller Memorial Prize. Junger, who converted to Catholicism at the age of 101, received a commendation from Pope John Paul II and was an honored guest of French President Francois Mitterrand and German Chancellor Helmut Kohl at the Franco-German reconciliation ceremony at Verdun in 1984.

---

1    Ian Buruma, "The Anarch at Twilight", *New York Review of Books*, Volume 40, No. 12, June 24, 1993. Hilary Barr, "An Exchange on Ernst Junger", *New York Review of Books*, Volume 40, No. 21, December 16, 1993.

Though he was an exceptional achiever during virtually every stage of his extraordinarily long life, it was his work during the Weimar period that not only secured for a Junger a presence in German cultural and political history, but also became the standard by which much of his later work was evaluated and by which his reputation was, and still is, debated.[2]

Ernst Junger was born on March 29, 1895 in Heidelberg, but was raised in Hanover. His father, also named Ernst, was an academically trained chemist who became wealthy as the owner of a pharmaceutical manufacturing business, finding he was successful enough to essentially retire while he was still in his forties. Though raised as an evangelical Protestant, Junger's father did not believe in any formal religion, nor did his mother, Karoline, an educated middle class German woman whose interests included Germany's rich literary tradition and the cause of women's emancipation. His parents' politics seem to have been liberal, though not radical, in the manner not uncommon to the rising bourgeoisie of Germany's upper middle class during the pre-war period. It was in this affluent, secure bourgeoisie environment that Ernst Junger grew up. Indeed, many of Junger's later activities and professed beliefs are easily understood as a revolt against the comfort and safety of his upbringing. As a child, he was an avid reader of the tales of adventurers and soldiers, but a poor academic student who did not adjust well to the regimented Prussian educational system. Junger's instructors consistently complained of his inattentiveness. As an adolescent, he became involved with the Wandervogel, roughly the German equivalent of the Boy Scouts.[3]

It was while attending a boarding school near his parents' home in 1913, at the age of seventeen, that Junger first demonstrated his first propensity for what might be called an "adventurist" way

---

2   Nevin, Thomas. *Ernst Junger and Germany: Into the Abyss*, 1914-1945. Durham, N.C.: Duke University Press, 1996, pp. 1-7. Loose, Gerhard. *Ernst Junger*. New York: Twayne Publishers, 1974, preface.

3   Nevin, pp. 9-26. Loose, p. 21

of life. With only six months left before graduation, Junger left school, leaving no word to his family as to his destination. Using money given to him for school-related fees and expenses to buy a firearm and a railroad ticket to Verdun, Junger subsequently enlisted in the French Foreign Legion, an elite military unit of the French armed forces that accepted enlistees of any nationality and had a reputation for attracting fugitives, criminals and career mercenaries. Junger had no intention of staying with the Legion. He only wanted to be posted to Africa, as he eventually was. Junger then deserted, only to be captured and sentenced to jail. Eventually his father found a capable lawyer for his wayward son and secured his release. Junger then returned to his studies and underwent a belated high school graduation. However, it was only a very short time later that Junger was back in uniform.[4]

## Warrior and War Diarist

Ernst Junger immediately volunteered for military service when he heard the news that Germany was at war in the summer of 1914. After two months of training, Junger was assigned to a reserve unit stationed at Champagne. He was afraid the war would end before he had the opportunity to see any action. This attitude was not uncommon among many recruits or conscripts who fought in the war for their respective states. The question immediately arises as to why so many young people would wish to look into the face of death with such enthusiasm. Perhaps they really did not understand the horrors that awaited them. In Junger's case, his rebellion against the security and luxury of his bourgeoisie upbringing had already been ably demonstrated by his excursion with the French Foreign Legion. Because of his high school education, something that soldiers of more proletarian origins lacked, Junger was selected to train to become an officer. Shortly before beginning his officer's training, Junger was exposed to combat for the first time. From the start, he carried pocket-sized notebooks with him and recorded his

---

4    Loose, p. 22. Nevin, pp. 27-37.

observations on the front lines. His writings while at the front exhibit a distinctive tone of detachment, as though he is simply an observer watching while the enemy fires at others. In the middle part of 1915, Junger suffered his first war wound, a bullet graze to the thigh that required only two weeks of recovery time. Afterwards, he was promoted to the rank of lieutenant.[5]

At age twenty-one, Junger was the leader of a reconnaissance team at the Somme whose purpose was to go out at night and search for British landmines. Early on, he acquired the reputation of a brave soldier who lacked the preoccupation with his own safety common to most of the fighting men. The introduction of steel artifacts into the war, tanks for the British side and steel helmets for the Germans, made a deep impression on Junger. Wounded three times at the Somme, Junger was awarded the Iron Medal First Class. Upon recovery, he returned to the front lines. A combat daredevil, he once held out against a much larger British force with only twenty men. After being transferred to fight the French at Flanders, he lost ten of his fourteen men and was wounded in the left hand by a blast from French shelling. After being harshly criticized by a superior officer for the number of men lost on that particular mission, Junger began to develop contempt for the military hierarchy whom he regarded as having achieved their status as a result of their class position, frequently lacking combat experience of their own. In late 1917, having already experienced nearly three full years of combat, Junger was wounded for the fifth time during a surprise assault by the British. He was grazed in the head by a bullet, acquiring two holes in his helmet in the process. His performance in this battle won him the Knights Cross of the Hohenzollerns. In March 1918, Junger participated in another fierce battle with the British, losing 87 of his 150 men.[6]

---

5    Nevin. p. 49.

6    *Ibid.*, p. 57

Nothing impressed Junger more than personal bravery and endurance on the part of soldiers. He once "fell to the ground in tears" at the sight of a young recruit who had only days earlier been unable to carry an ammunition case by himself suddenly being able to carry two cases of missiles after surviving an attack of British shells. A recurring theme in Junger's writings on his war experiences is the way in which war brings out the most savage human impulses. Essentially, human beings are given full license to engage in behavior that would be considered criminal during peacetime. He wrote casually about burning occupied towns during the course of retreat or a shift of position. However, Junger also demonstrated a capacity for merciful behavior during his combat efforts. He refrained from shooting a cornered British soldier after the foe displayed a portrait of his family to Junger. He was wounded yet again in August of 1918. Having been shot in the chest and directly through a lung, this was his most serious wound yet. After being hit, he still managed to shoot dead yet another British officer. As Junger was being carried off the battlefield on a stretcher, one of the stretcher carriers was killed by a British bullet. Another German soldier attempted to carry Junger on his back, but the soldier was shot dead himself and Junger fell to the ground. Finally, a medic recovered him and pulled him out of harm's way. This episode would be the end of his battle experiences during the Great War.[7]

# In Storms of Steel

Junger's keeping of his wartime diaries paid off quite well in the long run. They were to become the basis of his first and most famous book, *In Storms of Steel*, published in 1920. The title was given to the book by Junger himself, having found the phrase in an Old Icelandic saga. It was at the suggestion of his father that Junger first sought to have his wartime memoirs published. Initially, he found no takers, antiwar sentiment being extremely high in Germany at the time, until his father at last arranged

---

7    *Ibid.*, p. 61

to have the work published privately. *In Storms of Steel* differs considerably from similar works published by war veterans during the same era, such as Erich Maria Remarque's *All Quiet on the Western Front* and John Dos Passos' *Three Soldiers*. Junger's book reflects none of the disillusionment with war by those experienced in its horrors of the kind found in these other works. Instead, Junger depicted warfare as an adventure in which the soldier faced the highest possible challenge, a battle to the death with a mortal enemy. Though Junger certainly considered himself to be a patriot and, under the influence of Maurice Barres,[8] eventually became a strident German nationalist, his depiction of military combat as an idyllic setting where human wills face the supreme test rose far above ordinary nationalist sentiments. Junger's warrior ideal was not merely the patriot fighting out of a profound sense of loyalty to his country or the stereotype of the dutiful soldier whose sense of honor and obedience compels him to follow the orders of his superiors in a headlong march towards death. Nor was the warrior prototype exalted by Junger necessarily an idealist fighting for some alleged greater good such as a political ideal or religious devotion. Instead, war itself is the ideal for Junger. On this question, he was profoundly influenced by Nietzsche, whose dictum "a good war justifies any cause," provides an apt characterization of Junger's depiction of the life (and death) of the combat soldier.[9]

This aspect of Junger's outlook is illustrated quite well by the ending he chose to give to the first edition of *In Storms of Steel*. Although the second edition (published in 1926) ends with

---

8    Maurice Barrès (September 22, 1862 - December 4, 1923) was a French novelist, journalist, an anti-semite, nationalist politician and agitator. Leaning towards the far-left in his youth as a Boulangist deputy, he progressively developed a theory close to Romantic nationalism and shifted to the right during the Dreyfus Affair, leading the Anti-Dreyfusards alongside Charles Maurras. In 1906, he was elected both to the Académie française and as deputy of the Seine department, and until his death he sat with the conservative Entente républicaine démocratique. A strong supporter of the Union sacréi(Holy Union) during World War I, Barrès remained a major influence of generations of French writers, as well as of monarchists, although he was not a monarchist himself. 9. Nevin, pp. 58, 71, 97.

9    Nevin, pp. 58, 71, 97.

the nationalist rallying cry, "Germany lives and shall never go under!", a sentiment that was deleted for the third edition published in 1934 at the onset of the Nazi era, the original edition ends simply with Junger in the hospital after being wounded for the final time and receiving word that he has received yet another commendation for his valor as a combat soldier. There is no mention of Germany's defeat a few months later. Nationalism aside, the book is clearly about Junger, not about Germany, and Junger's depiction of the war simultaneously displays an extraordinary level of detachment for someone who lived in the face of death for four years and a highly personalized account of the war where battle is first and foremost about the assertion of one's own "will to power" with clichéd patriotic pieties being of secondary concern.

Indeed, Junger goes so far as to say there were winners and losers on both sides of the war. The true winners were not those who fought in a particular army or for a particular country, but who rose to the challenge placed before them and essentially achieved what Junger regarded as a higher state of enlightenment. He believed the war had revealed certain fundamental truths about the human condition. First, the illusions of the old bourgeoisie order concerning peace, progress and prosperity had been inalterably shattered. This was not an uncommon sentiment during that time, but it is a revelation that Junger seems to revel in while others found it to be overwhelmingly devastating. Indeed, the lifelong champion of Enlightenment liberalism, Bertrand Russell, whose life was almost as long as Junger's and who observed many of the same events from a much different philosophical perspective, once remarked that no one who had been born before 1914 knew what it was like to be truly happy.[10]

A second observation advanced by Junger had to do with the role of technology in transforming the nature of war, not only in a purely mechanical sense, but on a much greater existential level.

---

10  Schilpp, P. A. "The Philosophy of Bertrand Russell". Reviewed Hermann Weyl, *The American Mathematical Monthly*, Vol. 53, No. 4 (Apr., 1946), pp. 208-214.

Before, man had commanded weaponry in the course of combat. Now weaponry of the kind made possible by modern technology and industrial civilization essentially commanded man. The machines did the fighting. Man simply resisted this external domination. Lastly, the supremacy of might and the ruthless nature of human existence had been demonstrated. Nietzsche was right. The tragic, Darwinian nature of the human condition had been revealed as an irrevocable law.

*Storms of Steel* was the first of several works based on his experiences as a combat officer that were written by Junger during the 1920s. *Copse 125* described a battle between two small groups of combatants. In this work, Junger continued to explore the philosophical themes present in his first work. The type of technologically driven warfare that emerged during the Great War is characterized as reducing men to automatons driven by airplanes, tanks and machine guns. Once again, jingoistic nationalism is downplayed as a contributing factor to the essence of combat soldier's spirit. Another work of Junger's from the early 1920s, *Battle as Inner Experience*, explored the psychology of war. Junger suggested that civilization itself was but a mere mask for the "primordial" nature of humanity that once again reveals itself during war. Indeed, war had the effect of elevating humanity to a higher level. The warrior becomes a kind of god-like animal, divine in his superhuman qualities, but animalistic in his bloodlust. The perpetual threat of imminent death is a kind of intoxicant. Life is at its finest when death is closest. Junger described war as a struggle for a cause that overshadows the respective political or cultural ideals of the combatants. This overarching cause is courage. The fighter is honor bound to respect the courage of his mortal enemy. Drawing on the philosophy of Nietzsche, Junger argued that the war had produced a "new race" that had replaced the old pieties, such as those drawn from religion, with a new recognition of the primacy of the "will to power".[11]

---

11    Nevin, pp. 122, 125, 134, 136, 140, 173.

# Conservative Revolutionary

Junger's writings about the war quickly earned him the status of a celebrity during the Weimar period. *Battle as Inner Experience* contained the prescient suggestion that the young men who had experienced the greatest war the world had yet to see at that point could never be successfully re-integrated into the old bourgeoisie order from which they came. For these fighters, the war had been a spiritual experience. Having endured so much only to see their side lose on such seemingly humiliating terms, the veterans of the war were aliens to the rationalistic, anti-militarist, liberal republic that emerged in 1918 at the close of the war. Junger was at his parents' home recovering from war wounds during the time of the attempted coup by the leftist workers' and soldiers' councils and subsequent suppression of these by the Freikorps. He experimented with psychoactive drugs such as cocaine and opium during this time, something that he would continue to do much later in life. Upon recovery, he went back into active duty in the much diminished Germany army. Junger's earliest works, such as *In Storms of Steel*, were published during this time and he also wrote for military journals on the more technical and specialized aspects of combat and military technology. Interestingly, Junger attributed Germany's defeat in the war simply to poor leadership, both military and civilian, and rejected the "stab in the back" legend that consoled less keen veterans.

After leaving the army in 1923, Junger continued to write; producing a novella about a soldier during the war titled *Sturm*, and also began to study the philosophy of Oswald Spengler. His first work as a philosopher of nationalism appeared in the Nazi paper *Volkischer Beobachter* in September, 1923. Critiquing the failed Marxist revolution of 1918, Junger argued that the leftist coup failed because of its lacking of fresh ideas. It was simply a regurgitation of the egalitarian outlook of the French Revolution. The revolutionary left appealed only to the material wants of the Germany people in Junger's views. A successful revolution would have to be much more than that. It would have to appeal to their spiritual or "folkish" instincts as well.

Over the next few years Junger studied the natural sciences at the University of Leipzig and in 1925, at age thirty, he married nineteen-year-old Gretha von Jeinsen. Around this time, he also became a full-time political writer. Junger was hostile to Weimar democracy and its commercial bourgeoisie society. His emerging political ideal was one of an elite warrior caste that stood above petty partisan politics and the middle class obsession with material acquisition. Junger became involved with the the Stahlhelm, a right-wing veterans group, and was a contributor to its paper, *Die Standardite*. He associated himself with the younger, more militant members of the organization who favored an uncompromised nationalist revolution and eschewed the parliamentary system. Junger's weekly column in *Die Standardite* disseminated his nationalist ideology to his less educated readers. Junger's views at this point were a mixture of Spengler, Social Darwinism, and the traditionalist philosophy of the French rightist Maurice Barres, opposition to the internationalism of the left that had seemingly been discredited by the events of 1914, irrationalism and anti-parliamentarianism. He took a favorable view of the working class and praised the Nazis' efforts to win proletarian sympathies. Junger also argued that a nationalist outlook need not be attached to one particular form of government, even suggesting that a liberal monarchy would be inferior to a nationalist republic.[12]

In an essay for *Die Standardite* titled "The Machine," Junger argued that the principal struggle was not between social classes or political parties but between man and technology. He was not anti-technological in a Luddite sense, but regarded the technological apparatus of modernity to have achieved a position of superiority over mankind which needed to be reversed. He was concerned that the mechanized efficiency of modern life produced a corrosive effect on the human spirit. Junger considered the Nazis' glorification of peasant life to be antiquated. Ever the realist, he believed the world of the rural people to be in a state

---

12   Ibid., pp. 75-91.

of irreversible decline. Instead, Junger espoused a "metropolitan nationalism" centered on the urban working class. Nationalism was the antidote to the anti-particularist materialism of the Marxists who, in Junger's views, simply mirrored the liberals in their efforts to reduce the individual to a component of a mechanized mass society. The humanitarian rhetoric of the left Junger dismissed as the hypocritical cant of power-seekers feigning benevolence. He began to pin his hopes for a nationalist revolution on the younger veterans who comprised much of the urban working class.

In 1926, Junger became editor of *Arminius*, which also featured the writings of Nazi leaders like Alfred Rosenberg and Joseph Goebbels. In 1927, he contributed his final article to the Nazi paper, calling for a new definition of the "worker," one not rooted in Marxist ideology but the idea of the worker as a civilian counterpart to the soldier who struggles fervently for the nationalist ideal. Junger and Hitler had exchanged copies of their respective writings and a scheduled meeting between the two was canceled due to a change in Hitler's itinerary. Junger respected Hitler's abilities as an orator, but came to feel he lacked the ability to become a true leader. He also found Nazi ideology to be intellectually shallow, many of the Nazi movement's leaders to be talentless and was displeased by the vulgarity, crassly opportunistic and overly theatrical aspects of Nazi public rallies. Always an elitist, Junger considered the Nazis' pandering the common people to be debased. As he became more skeptical of the Nazis, Junger began writing for a wider circle of readers beyond that of the militant nationalist right-wing. His works began to appear in the Jewish liberal Leopold Schwarzchild's *Das Tagebuch* and the "national-Bolshevik" Ernst Niekisch's *Widerstand*.

Junger began to assemble around himself an elite corps of bohemian, eccentric intellectuals who would meet regularly on Friday evenings. This group included some of the most interesting personalities of the Weimar period. Among them were the Freikorps veteran Ernst von Salomon, Otto von Strasser, who with his brother Gregor led a leftist anti-Hitler faction of the Nazi movement, the national-Bolshevik Niekisch, the Jewish anarchist Erich Muhsam who had figured prominently in the early phase of the failed leftist revolution of 1918, the American writer Thomas Wolfe and the expressionist writer Arnolt Bronnen. Many among this group espoused a type of revolutionary socialism based on nationalism rather than class, disdaining the Nazis' opportunistic outreach efforts to the middle class. Some, like Niekisch, favored an alliance between Germany and Soviet Russia against the liberal-capitalist powers of the West. Occasionally, Joseph Goebbels would turn up at these meetings hoping to convert the group, particularly Junger himself, whose war writings he had admired, to the Nazi cause. These efforts by the Nazi propaganda master proved unsuccessful. Junger regarded Goebbels as a shallow ideologue who spoke in platitudes even in private conversation.[13]

The final break between Ernst Junger and the NSDAP occurred in September 1929. Junger published an article in Schwarzchild's *Tagebuch* attacking and ridiculing the Nazis as sell outs for having reinvented themselves as a parliamentary party. He also dismissed their racism and anti-Semitism as ridiculous, stating that according to the Nazis a nationalist is simply someone who "eats three Jews for breakfast." He condemned the Nazis for pandering to the liberal middle class and reactionary traditional conservatives "with lengthy tirades against the decline in morals, against abortion, strikes, lockouts, and the reduction of police and military forces." Goebbels responded by attacking Junger in the Nazi press, accusing him being motivated by personal literary ambition, and insisting this had caused him "to vilify the national socialist movement, probably so as to make himself popular in his new kosher surroundings" and dismissing Junger's attacks by proclaiming the Nazis did not "debate with renegades who abuse us in the smutty press of Jewish traitors."[14]

---

13    Ibid., p. 107.

14    Ibid., p. 108.

## Junger on the Jewish Question

Junger held complicated views on the question of German Jews. He considered anti-Semitism of the type espoused by Hitler to be crude and reactionary. Yet his own version of nationalism required a level of homogeneity that was difficult to reconcile with the sub national status of Germany Jewry. Junger suggested that Jews should assimilate and pledge their loyalty to Germany once and for all. Yet he expressed admiration for Orthodox Judaism and indifference to Zionism. Junger maintained personal friendships with Jews and wrote for a Jewish owned publication. During this time his Jewish publisher Schwarzchild published an article examining Junger's views on the Jews of Germany. Schwarzchild insisted that Junger was nothing like his Nazi rivals on the far right. Junger's nationalism was based on an aristocratic warrior ethos, while Hitler's was more comparable to the criminal underworld. Hitler's men were "plebian alley scum". However, Schwarzchild also characterized Junger's rendition of nationalism as motivated by little more than a fervent rejection of bourgeoisie society and lacking in attention to political realities and serious economic questions.[15]

## The Worker

Other than *In Storms of Steel*, Junger's *The Worker: Mastery and Form* was his most influential work from the Weimar era. Junger would later distance himself from this work, published in 1932, and it was reprinted in the 1950s only after Junger was prompted to do so by Martin Heidegger.

In *The Worker*, Junger outlines his vision of a future state ordered as a technocracy based on workers and soldiers led by warrior elite. Workers are no longer simply components of an industrial machine, whether capitalist or communist, but have become a kind of civilian-soldier operating as an economic warrior. Just as the soldier glories in his accomplishments in battle, so does the

---

15    Ibid., pp. 109-111.

worker glory in the achievements expressed through his work. Junger predicted that continued technological advancements would render the worker/capitalist dichotomy obsolete. He also incorporated the political philosophy of his friend Carl Schmitt into his worldview. As Schmitt saw international relations as a Hobbesian battle between rival powers, Junger believed each state would eventually adopt a system not unlike what he described in *The Worker*. Each state would maintain its own technocratic order with the workers and soldiers of each country playing essentially the same role on behalf of their respective nations. International affairs would be a crucible where the will to power of the different nations would be tested.

Junger's vision contains certain amount prescience. The general trend in politics at the time was a movement towards the kind of technocratic state Junger described. These took on many varied forms including German National Socialism, Italian Fascism, Soviet Communism, the growing welfare states of Western Europe and America's New Deal. Coming on the eve of World War Two, Junger's prediction of a global Hobbesian struggle between national collectives possessing previously unimagined levels of technological sophistication also seems rather prophetic. Junger once again attacked the bourgeoisie as anachronistic. Its values of material luxury and safety he regarded as unfit for the violent world of the future.[16]

# The National Socialist Era

By the time Hitler came to power in 1933, Junger's war writings had become commonly used in high schools and universities as examples of wartime literature, and Junger enjoyed success within the context of German popular culture as well. Excerpts of Junger's works were featured in military journals. The Nazis tried to co-opt his semi-celebrity status, but he was uncooperative. Junger was appointed to the Nazified German

---

16    Ibid., pp. 114-140.

Academy of Poetry, but declined the position. When the Nazi Party's paper published some of his work in 1934, Junger wrote a letter of protest. The Nazi regime, despite its best efforts to capitalize on his reputation, viewed Junger with suspicion. His past association with the national-Bolshevik Ersnt Niekisch, the Jewish anarchist Erich Muhsam and the anti-Hitler Nazi Otto von Strasser, all of whom were either eventually killed or exiled by the Third Reich, led the Nazis to regard Junger as a potential subversive. On several occasions, Junger received visits from the Gestapo in search of some of his former friends. During the early years of the Nazi regime, Junger was in the fortunate position of being able to economically afford travel outside of Germany. He journeyed to Norway, Brazil, Greece and Morocco during this time, and published several works based on his travels.[17]

Junger's most significant work from the Nazi period is the novel *On the Marble Cliffs*. The book is an allegorical attack on the Hitler regime. It was written in 1939, the same year that Junger reentered the German army. The book describes a mysterious villain that threatens a community, a sinister warlord called the "Head Ranger". This character is never featured in the plot of the novel, but maintains a foreboding presence that is universal (much like "Big Brother" in George Orwell's *1984*). Another character in the novel, "Braquemart", is described as having physical characteristics remarkably similar to those of Goebbels. The book sold fourteen thousand copies during its first two weeks in publication. Swiss reviewers immediately recognized the allegorical references to the Nazi state in the novel. The Nazi Party's organ, *Volkische Beobachter*, stated that Ernst Jünger was flirting with a bullet to the head. Goebbels urged Hitler to ban the book, but Hitler refused, probably not wanting to show his hand. Indeed, Hitler gave orders that Junger not be harmed.[18]

---

17    Ibid., p. 145.

18    Ibid., p. 162.

Junger was stationed in France for most of the Second World War. Once again, he kept diaries of the experience. Once again, he expressed concern that he might not get to see any action before the war was over. While Junger did not have the opportunity to experience the level of danger and daredevil heroics he had during the Great War, he did receive yet another medal, the Iron Cross, for retrieving the body of a dead corporal while under heavy fire. Junger also published some of his war diaries during this time. However, the German government took a dim view of these, viewing them as too sympathetic to the occupied French. Junger's duties included censorship of the mail coming into France from German civilians. He took a rather liberal approach to this responsibility and simply disposed of incriminating documents rather than turning them over for investigation. In doing so, he probably saved lives. He also encountered members of France's literary and cultural elite, among them the actor Louis Ferdinand Celine, a raving anti-Semite and pro-Vichyite who suggested Hitler's harsh measures against the Jews had not been heavy handed enough. As rumors of the Nazi extermination programs began to spread, Junger wrote in his diary that the mechanization of the human spirit of the type he had written about in the past had apparently generated a higher level of human depravity. When he saw three young French-Jewish girls wearing the yellow stars required by the Nazis, he wrote that he felt embarrassed to be in the Nazi army. In July of 1942, Junger observed the mass arrest of French Jews, the beginning of implementation of the "Final Solution." He described the scene as follows:

> "Parents were first separated from their children, so there was wailing to be heard in the streets. At no moment may I forget that I am surrounded by the unfortunate, by those suffering to the very depths, else what sort of person, what sort of officer would I be? The uniform obliges one to grant protection wherever it goes. Of course one has the impression that one must also, like Don Quixote, take on millions."[19]

---

19    Ibid., p. 189.

An entry into Junger's diary from October 16, 1943 suggests that an unnamed army officer had told Junger about the use of crematoria and poison gas to murder Jews *en masse*. Rumors of plots against Hitler circulated among the officers with whom Junger maintained contact. His son, Ernst, was arrested after an informant claimed he had spoken critically of Hitler. Ernst Junger was imprisoned for three months then placed in a penal battalion where he was killed in action in Italy. On July 20, 1944 an unsuccessful assassination attempt was carried out against Hitler. It is still disputed as to whether or not Junger knew of the plot or had a role in its planning. Among those arrested for their role in the attempt on Hitler's life were members of Junger's immediate circle of associates and superior officers within the German army. Junger was dishonorably discharged shortly afterward.[20]

Following the close of the Second World War, Junger came under suspicion from the Allied occupational authorities because of his far right-wing nationalist and militarist past. He refused to cooperate with the Allies De-Nazification programs and was barred from publishing for four years. He would go on to live another half century, producing many more literary works, becoming a close friend of Albert Hoffman, the inventor of the hallucinogen LSD, with which he experimented. In a 1977 novel, *Eumeswil*, he took his tendency towards viewing the world around him with detachment to a newer, more clearly articulated level with his invention of the concept of the "Anarch". This idea, heavily influenced by the writings of the early nineteenth century German philosopher Max Stirner, championed the solitary individual who remains true to himself within the context of whatever external circumstances happen to be present.

Some sample quotations from this work illustrate the philosophy and worldview of the elderly Junger quite well:

---

20    Ibid., p. 209.

"For the anarch, if he remains free of being ruled, whether by sovereign or society, this does not mean he refuses to serve in any way. In general, he serves no worse than anyone else, and sometimes even better, if he likes the game. He only holds back from the pledge, the sacrifice, the ultimate devotion ... I serve in the Casbah; if, while doing this, I die for the Condor, it would be an accident, perhaps even an obliging gesture, but nothing more."

"The egalitarian mania of demagogues is even more dangerous than the brutality of men in galooned coats. For the anarch, this remains theoretical, because he avoids both sides. Anyone who has been oppressed can get back on his feet if the oppression did not cost him his life. A man who has been equalized is physically and morally ruined. Anyone who is different is not equal; that is one of the reasons why the Jews are so often targeted."

"The anarch, recognizing no government, but not indulging in paradisal dreams as the anarchist does, is, for that very reason, a neutral observer."

"Opposition is collaboration."

"A basic theme for the anarch is how man, left to his own devices, can defy superior force - whether state, society or the elements - by making use of their rules without submitting to them."

"... malcontents... prowl through the institutions eternally dissatisfied, always disappointed. Connected with this is their love of cellars and rooftops, exile and prisons, and also banishment, on which they actually pride themselves. When the structure finally caves in they are the first to be killed in the collapse. Why do they not know that the world remains inalterable in change? Because they never find their way down to its real depth, their own. That is the sole place of essence, safety. And so they do themselves in."

"The anarch may not be spared prisons - as one fluke of existence among others. He will then find the fault in himself."

"We are touching one a ... distinction between anarch and anarchist; the relation to authority, to legislative power. The anarchist is their mortal enemy, while the anarch refuses to acknowledge them. He seeks neither to gain hold of them, nor to topple them, nor to alter them - their impact bypasses him. He must resign himself only to the whirlwinds they generate."

"The anarch is no individualist, either. He wishes to present himself neither as a Great Man nor as a Free Spirit. His own measure is enough for him; freedom is not his goal; it is his property. He does not come on as foe or reformer: one can get along nicely with him in shacks or in palaces. Life is too short and too beautiful to sacrifice for ideas, although contamination is not always avoidable. But hats off to the martyrs."

"We can expect as little from society as from the state. Salvation lies in the individual."[21]

---

21    Junger, Ernst. *Eumeswil.* New York: Marion Publishers, 1980, 1993.

# *Carl Schmitt*

## Carl Schmitt and the Nomos of the Earth

Carl Schmitt was without question one of the most important political philosophers and legal theorists of the 20<sup>th</sup> century. During his extraordinarily long life, Schmitt wrote on public affairs over a period of about 70 years. He began writing during the period before WWI, and went on to observe the events of the First World War, the interwar period, WW2, the postwar and Cold War eras, and he eventually died the same year that Mikhail Gorbachev became the last Soviet head of state. It was through the process of observing the unfolding of all of these events, that Schmitt developed his very comprehensive system of thought. Given the length of Schmitt's career as a political writer as well as the scope and depth of his thought, it would of course be impossible to do justice to the ideas of Carl Schmitt in a brief presentation here today. So what I want to focus on primarily are those aspects of Schmitt's thinking that are most relevant to our current political situation and the questions and issues that many of us are the most concerned with. Schmitt was first and foremost a staunch political realist in the tradition of Hobbes and Machiavelli. Given the foundations and presumptions behind his thought, it should not surprise us that Schmitt was primarily concerned with the question of how order is to be maintained on both an international level and within the context of the internal affairs of particular nations as well, and much of his writing throughout his life is devoted to a brutally honest and penetrating examination of these questions. With our own benefit of hindsight, we can see how prescient Schmitt's thinking often was on so many different matters.

The question of the state was always at the forefront of Schmitt's thinking. Like Max Weber, Schmitt considered the state's claim of a monopoly on the legitimate use of violence to be the defining characteristic of the modern state. Schmitt regarded the state's development of a monopoly on warfare as one of the great achievements of European civilization as, in his view, this had the effect of civilizing war. Throughout his life, Schmitt persistently expressed concern about the decline of the nation-state system and the implications of this for international order. Schmitt understood international law to be a distinctively European creation that had its roots in both the achievement of European dominance on a worldwide basis beginning with the Age of Discovery *and* with the emergence of the Peace of Westphalia and its system of sovereign nation-states at the conclusion of the Thirty Years War in 1648. It is also important for our purposes to understand that the traditional European conception of international law involved a body of law that was customary in nature and was rooted in a shared consensus among European nations and was not something that was cultivated or enforced by any sort of overarching institutional entity.

Schmitt understood that traditional European international law had essentially been destroyed by the events of the First World War, the imposition of the Versailles Treaty on Germany, and the emergence of the League of Nations. It was these events that shifted the foundations of international law from its Eurocentric origins to a foundation that was universalist in nature. Along with these developments came the end of European domination and the rise of American dominance due to the role of the United States in shifting the European balance of power in the First World War and the subsequent creation of the League of Nations. Schmitt regarded the rise of the United States as a major world power to be significant in two principal ways. First, American imperialism tended to be primarily economic in nature as opposed to the more overtly political forms that European imperialism had previously assumed. Secondly, American intervention in the First World War had introduced the concept of war as an instrument of ideology into international law. Under the older European system, war had been regarded primarily as an instrument of policy with its focus being on limited territorial interests or geopolitical aims. With President Woodrow Wilson's declaration of American involvement in World War One to be a "war to end all wars" or a war to "make the world safe for democracy," war once again took on the form of a crusade just as it had during the Middle Ages. When war is conceived of in this way, then the enemy becomes not merely an adversary to be defeated but is instead regarded as moral reprobate to be annihilated. Under such conditions, war becomes much more total in nature and much more destructive.

Schmitt continued to develop this thesis as he observed the unfolding of the events of the twentieth century. As the traditional European conception of international law within a framework of sovereign nation-states began to recede, Schmitt felt there were two potential alternatives that would replace the European tradition. One of these was the universalism favored by the Americans, which was rooted in the idea that there is some moral obligation to bring the supposed virtues of modern democracy to the entire world and that it is the responsibility of what is now called the "international community" to enforce Western liberal standards of "human rights" on a global scale. Of course, the institutional manifestation of this idea was originally the League of Nations during the interwar period and then the United Nations in the postwar era. Against this globalizing universalism, Schmitt proposed the concept of "political pluralism" which was the idea that regional powers would retain sovereignty over their own spheres of influence. Ironically, Schmitt cited the Monroe Doctrine as a prototype for the kind of international political pluralism that he envisioned. Under such a system, each regional power would maintain something resembling its own Monroe Doctrine. Not surprisingly, then, Schmitt regarded the rise of the bipolar order of the Cold War period as a favorable alternative to universal American hegemony in spite of the fact that Schmitt was always a strong opponent of communism.

Now, a lot of Schmitt's views on this question were obviously rooted in his own antipathy towards the United States. First, there was the role of the United States in Germany's defeat in World War One and the subsequent imposition of the Versailles Treaty. Second, there were the American aerial assaults on German cities during the Second World War. Lastly, there was Schmitt's own imprisonment at the hands of the Americans as a potential war criminal due to his previous collaboration with the National Socialists immediately following World War Two. However, it is still quite interesting that Schmitt actually regarded the United States as a more ideologically-driven state than the Soviet Union in the sense that the Soviets in their occupation of Germany simply behaved as an ordinary conquering power while it was the Americans that Schmitt found to be much more concerned about the imposition of ideological purity.

This observation by Schmitt contributes a great deal towards our understanding of the role of American power in creating the global order that has emerged since the end of the Cold War. Many critics of contemporary American foreign policy, from both the Left and the Right, will often focus on the role of either material or economic interests in the shaping of U.S. foreign policy. A standard illustration of that is the interpretation of the American wars in Iraq or Afghanistan or Libya as simply being wars for oil or a gas pipeline or something along those lines. That interpretation is fairly typical among leftists and we've all seen the placards that are displayed at left-wing antiwar rallies with slogans like "No Blood for Oil" and there are also some on the Right who hold similar views. There are others who interpret American militarism in the post-Cold War era as simply being about the maintenance of the vested interests associated with the military-industrial complex or, alternately, as being driven by narrow demographic interests. As an example of the latter, American intervention in the Middle East will be interpreted as being driven primarily by the influence of the Israel lobby in domestic American politics. But while there is likely some degree of truth to all of these claims, it would be a mistake to ignore or minimize the role that ideology plays in the shaping of American foreign policy.

The two prevailing ideological frameworks that American foreign policy elites subscribe to are either liberal internationalism on one hand or the neoconservative perspective on the other. Liberal internationalism is, of course, the idea that liberal states should intervene in the affairs of other states in order to achieve liberal ideological objectives. And while neo-conservatism is often considered to be a manifestation of the Right by more mainstream political observers, if anything neo-conservatism is an even more extreme and ideologically-driven approach to foreign policy in that it advocates exporting Western notions of liberal democracy to the entire globe by means of not only military intervention, but also through the radical reconstruction of entire societies. In other words, neo-conservatism is an "armed doctrine" of the kind criticized by Edmund Burke.

As an illustration of the contrast Carl Schmitt identified between foreign policy as it might be pursued by an ideologically-driven state and foreign policy as it might be pursued in the more traditional European sense of simply upholding territorial or geopolitical interests, we can consider what the American approach to its more recent wars might have been if American foreign policy were less ideological in nature and more Schmittian instead. Just for purposes of discussion and without making any broader judgments about military interventions by the United States over the past decade, it is certainly conceivable that policy makers operating within a non-ideological framework of traditional power politics might come to regard, for instance, someone like Saddam Hussein or the former Taliban regime in Afghanistan, or Colonel Qadaffi as an enemy whose elimination was necessary or justifiable on the basis of a rational assessment of American interests. But within such a framework the much more ambitious and implausible projects of reconstructing Middle Eastern or Central Asian societies on the model of a Western liberal democracy would be absent. Consequentially, these recent American wars would have been far less costly to the United States in terms of blood and treasure and in all probability less costly to the other nations involved as well. For instance, there would have been much less need for the sustained military occupations that have resulted from some of those interventions.

A phrase that Schmitt coined to describe the workings of an ideologically-driven state was the "tyranny of values." With this concept of the "tyranny of values," Schmitt was describing two very distinct but interrelated types of political phenomena that he saw as endemic to the types of states that were emerging in his own time. The first of these phenomena was what I have been describing thus far, and that is the scenario whereby international relations and the nature of warfare between states began to shift from an orientation from the pursuit of more limited territorial interests towards the pursuit of ideological crusades. The second of these was the way in which ideologically driven movements perpetually created disorder by attempting to overthrow traditional institutions in order to reconstruct societies according to prescriptive ideological values. This latter point is very strongly related to Carl Schmitt's critique of modern liberal democracies of the kind that came to dominate Western nations in the 20th century.

Indeed, I believe that one of the most valuable aspects of Schmitt's thinking as it relates to our own time is his critique of the liberal democratic manifestation of the state. According to the political narrative that dominates contemporary thinking, the concept of liberal democracy is regarded as something that is sacrosanct. At the more extreme, we have the example of thinkers like Francis Fukuyama who considered the universal realization of conventional American-style or Western European-style liberal democracy, or "democratic capitalism" as the neoconservatives call it, as the final end of human political evolution and as some ultimate kind of human achievement. Extreme interpretations of this idea aside, some variation of this line of thought dominates virtually all of our present day institutions and intellectual life. The conventional narrative that we hear from contemporary institutions that serve to shape the ideological values that guide the broader society, whether our educational institutions, or the mass media, or the state itself, is one where Western history is presented as following this linear, progressive pattern towards ever greater levels of freedom, social justice, human rights, tolerance, inclusiveness, and all of these other contemporary pieties. The establishment and large scale realization of the liberal democratic conception of the state is regarded as being one of the hallmark achievements in this process of social and political evolution.

Carl Schmitt was one of a number of now-forgotten thinkers who criticized mass democracy of the kind associated with the modern liberal state as a degeneration of human political life. Far from granting greater freedom, for instance, Schmitt saw the democratic state as having the effect of completely politicizing the entire society. A state that is organized as a mass democracy continually tries to cultivate new constituencies for itself, which in turn means that new political interests continually arise that make demands that the state tries to satisfy. The end result of this is that the state ends up intervening in virtually every aspect of social, cultural, and economic life in order to capitulate to all of these constituencies. In other words, mass democracy in practice becomes a form of soft totalitarianism.

The other side of this coin is that while democracy may actually bring with it a decrease in freedom, it also brings a decrease in social cohesion and political order that ultimately threatens its own survival. Schmitt understood that mass democracy of the kind that has come to be practiced in modern societies is ultimately nothing more than a permanent war of special interest groups that are trying to gain control over the state. In the process, the state actually begins to lose legitimacy because by trying to be everything to everyone, the state ends up satisfying no one.

Another essential aspect of Schmitt's thought is his concept of the friend/enemy distinction and his identification of what he considered to be the essence of the "political." According to Schmitt, the fundamental characteristic of what is meant by the political is the existence of organized collectives that pose a potential existential threat to one another and therefore have the potential to engage in lethal conflict. There does not have to be actual lethal conflict, but the possibility has to be present. The way that this idea of the "political" as Schmitt defined it relates to his critique of liberal democracy is through his recognition of the inability of the liberal state to recognize its own enemies or to act decisively against it enemies. In his own time, Schmitt was writing within the context of the Weimar Republic and criticizing what he saw as two fatal flaws in the liberal republic's approach to statecraft. One of these was the inability of the republic to act effectively in defense of Germany's national interests within the context of international power politics. The other was the inability of the republic to maintain domestic order within Germany and, in particular, to resist the existential threats posed to itself by the rising Nazi and Communist movements that were threatening the Weimar regime with overthrow either through the manipulation of the legal and political machinery or through extra-legal acts of violence.

The two developments of our own time where I think the ideas of Carl Schmitt are most relevant are the loss of the state's monopoly on warfare through the emergence of so-called "fourth generation warfare" whereby war is increasingly being waged by non-state actors, whether these be terrorist groups, drug cartels, gangs, cults, religious movements, guerrilla armies, or whatever, and where such entities supersede states in their claims of legitimacy or on the allegiance of their adherents or subordinates. Perhaps the best example of what I am talking about is Hezbollah, which has essentially replaced the Lebanese state as the guardian of the nation of Lebanon and arguably has more legitimacy than the Lebanese state itself. Contemporary military theorists like Martin Van Creveld and Bill Lind have written a great deal about the state's loss of its traditional monopoly on war that the rise of the fourth generation forces reflects. What this means is that

Schmitt's definition of the political as the potential for lethal violence between collectives that pose an existential threat to one another now applies not only to wars between states, but also to wars between non-state actors, or between states and non-state actors.

The other important development where Schmitt's thinking is particularly relevant is the inability of Western liberal states at present to recognize the existential threat to their own societies and broader civilization posed by the prospect of demographic overrun generated by mass immigration. This existential threat is developing and escalating even as some Western states are becoming more repressive with regards to traditional civil liberties. For instance, Sam Francis once pointed out the astonishing fact that after the events of September 11, 2001, it became the conventional wisdom among policy makers that in order to safeguard against terrorism, it was permissible to engage in torture or prolonged detention without trial, or to maintain secret prisons or establish military tribunals in place of civilian courts, but it was somehow not acceptable to simply eliminate immigration from places where potential terrorists are likely to originate. So what we see is a situation where a liberal state is on one hand completely ineffective even at safeguarding its own borders, yet at the same time, it has no problem casually throwing off long established constitutional traditions or extending the hand of the state into previously forbidden areas.

Another aspect of this question is the fact that so many liberal intellectuals fail to perceive the existential threat posed to the values they claim to cherish most by mass immigration from the Third World due to the fact that the preservation of the kind of hyper-liberal values that most contemporary intellectuals take for granted are simply not compatible with the importation of large numbers of people for whom such values are alien to their own cultural and national traditions. So as we observe all of these contemporary events, we can also see how the thinking of Carl Schmitt is still quite relevant to our time and has much to say regarding our own situation.

# The Political Theory of Carl Schmitt

The editors of *The Weimar Republic Sourcebook* attempt to summarize the political thought of Carl Schmitt and interpret his writings on political and legal theory on the basis of his later association with Nazism between 1933 and 1936. Schmitt is described as having "attempted to drive a wedge between liberalism and democracy and undercut the assumption that rational discourse and legal formalism could be the basis of political legitimacy."[1] His contributions to political theory are characterized as advancing the view that "genuine politics was irreducible to socio-economic conflicts and unconstrained by normative considerations". The essence of politics is a battle to the death "between friend and foe." The editors recognize distinctions between the thought of Schmitt and that of right-wing revolutionaries of Weimar, but assert that his ideas "certainly provided no obstacle to Schmitt's opportunistic embrace of Nazism."

As ostensible support for this interpretation of Schmitt, the editors provide excerpts from two of Schmitt's works. The first excerpt is from the preface to the second edition of Schmitt's *The Crisis of Parliamentary Democracy*, a work first published in 1923 with the preface having been written for the 1926 edition. In this excerpt, Schmitt describes the dysfunctional workings of the Weimar parliamentary system. He regards this dysfunction as symptomatic of the inadequacies of the classical liberal theory of government. According to this theory as Schmitt interprets it, the affairs of states are to be conducted on the basis of open discussion between proponents of competing ideas as a kind of empirical process. Schmitt contrasts this idealized view of parliamentarianism with the realities of its actual practice, such as cynical appeals by politicians to narrow self-interests on the part of constituents, bickering among narrow partisan forces, the use of propaganda and symbolism rather than rational discourse as a means of influencing public opinion, the binding of parliamentarians by party discipline, decisions made by means of backroom deals, rule by committee and so forth.

---

1    *Sourcebook*, p. 331

Schmitt recognizes a fundamental distinction between liberalism, or "parliamentarianism", and democracy. Liberal theory advances the concept of a state where all retain equal political rights. Schmitt contrasts this with actual democratic practice as it has existed historically. Historic democracy rests on an "equality of equals", for instance, those holding a particular social position (as in ancient Greece), subscribing to particular religious beliefs or belonging to a specific national entity. Schmitt observes that democratic states have traditionally included a great deal of political and social inequality, from slavery to religious exclusionism to a stratified class hierarchy. Even modern democracies ostensibly organized on the principle of universal suffrage do not extend such democratic rights to residents of their colonial possessions. Beyond this level, states, even officially "democratic" ones, distinguish between their own citizens and those of other states.

At a fundamental level, there is an innate tension between liberalism and democracy. Liberalism is individualistic, whereas democracy sanctions the "general will" as the principle of political legitimacy. However, a consistent or coherent "general will" necessitates a level of homogeneity that by its very nature goes against the individualistic ethos of liberalism. This is the source of the "crisis of parliamentarianism" that Schmitt suggests. According to the democratic theory rooted in the ideas of Jean Jacques Rousseau, a legitimate state must reflect the "general will", but no general will can be discerned in a regime that simultaneously espouses liberalism. Lacking the homogeneity necessary for a democratic "general will", the state becomes fragmented into competing interests. Indeed, a liberal parliamentary state can actually act against the "peoples' will" and become undemocratic. By this same principle, anti-liberal states such as those organized according to the principles of fascism or bolshevism can be democratic in so far as they reflect the "general will."

The second excerpt included by the editors is drawn from Schmitt's *The Concept of the Political*, published in 1927. According to Schmitt, the irreducible minimum on which human political life is based is the friend/enemy distinction. This friend/enemy distinction is to politics what the good/evil dichotomy is to morality, beautiful/ugly to aesthetics, profitable/unprofitable to economics, and so forth. These categories need not be inclusive of one another. For instance, a political enemy need not be morally evil or aesthetically ugly. What is significant is that the enemy is the "other" and therefore a source of possible conflict. The friend/enemy distinction is not dependent on the specific nature of the "enemy". It is merely enough that the enemy is a threat. The political enemy is also distinctive from personal enemies. Whatever one's personal thoughts about the political enemy, it remains true that the enemy is hostile to the collective to which one belongs. The first purpose of the state is to maintain its own existence as an organized collective prepared if necessary to do battle to the death with other organized collectives that pose an existential threat. This is the essential core of what is meant by the "political". Organized collectives within a particular state can also engage in such conflicts (i.e., civil war). Internal conflicts within a collective can threaten the survival of the collective as a whole. As long as existential threats to a collective remain, the friend/enemy concept that Schmitt considers to be the heart of politics will remain valid.

An implicit view of the ideas of Carl Schmitt can be distinguished from the editors' introductory comments and selective quotations from these two works. Is Schmitt attempting to "drive a wedge" between liberalism and democracy thereby undermining the Weimar regime's claims to legitimacy and pave the way for a more overtly authoritarian system? Is Schmitt arguing for a more exclusionary form of the state, for instance one that might practice exclusivity on ethnic or national grounds? Is Schmitt attempting to sanction the use of war as a mere political instrument, independent of any normative considerations, perhaps even as an ideal unto itself? If the answer to any of these questions is an affirmative one, then one might be able to plausibly argue that Schmitt is indeed creating a kind of intellectual framework that could later be used to justify at least some of the ideas of Nazism and even lead to an embrace of Nazism by Schmitt himself.

It would appear that the expression "context is everything" becomes a quite relevant when examining the work of Carl Schmitt. It is clear enough that the excerpts from Schmitt included in the *The Weimar Republic Sourcebook* have been chosen rather selectively. As a glaring example, this important passage from second edition's preface from *The Crisis of Parliamentary Democracy* has been deleted:

"That the parliamentary enterprise today is the lesser evil, that it will continue to be preferable to Bolshevism and dictatorship, that it would have unforeseen consequences were it to be discarded, that it is 'socially and technically' a very practical thing - all these are interesting and in part also correct observations. But they do not constitute the intellectual foundations of a specifically intended institution. Parliamentarianism exists today as a method of government and a political system. Just as everything else that exists and functions tolerably, it is useful - no more and no less. It counts for a great deal that even today it functions better than other untried methods, and that a minimum of order that is today actually at hand would be endangered by frivolous experiments. Every reasonable person would concede such arguments. But they do not carry weight in an argument about principles. Certainly no one would be so un-demanding that he regarded an intellectual foundation or a moral truth as proven by the question, "What else?" [2]

This passage, conspicuously absent from the *Sourcebook* excerpt, indicates that Schmitt is in fact wary of the idea of undermining

---

2    Schmitt, *Crisis,* pp. 2-3

the authority of the Republic for its own sake or for the sake of implementing a revolutionary regime. Schmitt is clearly a "conservative" in the tradition of Hobbes, one who values order and stability above all else, and also Burke, expressing a preference for the established, the familiar, the traditional, and the practical, and an aversion to extremism, fanaticism, utopianism, and upheaval for the sake of exotic ideological inclinations. Clearly, it would be rather difficult to reconcile such an outlook with the political millenarianism of either Marxism or National Socialism. The "crisis of parliamentary democracy" that Schmitt is addressing is a crisis of legitimacy. On what political or ethical principles does a liberal democratic state of the type Weimar purports to be claim and establish its own legitimacy? This is an immensely important question, given the gulf between liberal theory and parliamentary democracy as it is actually being practiced in Weimar, the conflicts between liberal practice and democratic theories of legitimacy as they have previously been laid out by Rousseau and others and, perhaps most importantly, the challenges to liberalism and claims to "democratic" legitimacy being made by proponents of totalitarian ideologies from both the Left and Right.

The introduction to the first edition and first chapter of *Crisis* contain a frank discussion of both the intellectual as well as practical problems associated with the practice of "democracy". Schmitt observes how democracy, broadly defined, has triumphed over older systems, such as monarchy, aristocracy or theocracy in favor of the principle of "popular sovereignty". However, the advent of democracy has also undermined older theories on the foundations of political legitimacy, such as those rooted in religion ("divine right of kings"), dynastic lineages or mere appeals to tradition. Further, the triumphs of both liberalism and democracy have brought into fuller view the innate conflicts between the two. There is also the additional matter of the gap between the practice of politics (such as parliamentary procedures) and the ends of politics (such as the "will of the people"). Schmitt observes how parliamentarianism as a procedural methodology has a wide assortment of critics, including those representing the forces of reaction (royalists and clerics, for instance) and radicalism (from Marxists to anarchists). Schmitt also points out that he is by no means the first thinker to point out these issues, citing Mosca, Jacob Burckhardt, Belloc, Chesterton, and Michels, among others.

A fundamental question that concerns Schmitt is the matter of what the democratic "will of the people" actually means, observing that an ostensibly democratic state could adopt virtually any set of policy positions, "whether militarist or pacifist, absolutist or liberal, centralized or decentralized, progressive or reactionary, and again at different times without ceasing to be a democracy."[3] He also raises the question of the fate of democracy in a society where "the people" cease to favor democracy. Can democracy be formally renounced in the name of democracy? For instance, can "the people" embrace Bolshevism or a fascist dictatorship as an expression of their democratic "general will"? The flip side of this question asks whether a political class committed in theory to democracy can act undemocratically (against "the will of the people") if the people display an insufficient level of education in the ways of democracy. How is the will of the people to be identified in the first place? Is it not possible for rulers to construct a "will of the people" of their own through the use of propaganda? For Schmitt, these questions are not simply a matter of intellectual hair-splitting but are of vital importance in a weak, politically paralyzed democratic state where the commitment of significant sectors of both the political class and the public at large to the preservation of democracy is questionable, and where the overthrow of democracy by proponents of other ideologies is a very real possibility.

Schmitt examines the claims of parliamentarianism to democratic legitimacy. He describes the liberal ideology that underlies parliamentarianism as follows:

---

3    Schmitt, *Crisis,* p. 25

"It is essential that liberalism be understood as a consistent, comprehensive metaphysical system. Normally one only discusses the economic line of reasoning that social harmony and the maximization of wealth follow from the free economic competition of individuals...But all this is only an application of a general liberal principle...: That truth can be found through an unrestrained clash of opinion and that competition will produce harmony." [4]

For Schmitt, this view reduces truth to "a mere function of the eternal competition of opinions." After pointing out the startling contrast between the theory and practice of liberalism, Schmitt suggests that liberal parliamentarian claims to legitimacy are rather weak and examines the claims of rival ideologies. Marxism replaces the liberal emphasis on the competition between opinions with a focus on competition between economic classes and, more generally, differing modes of production that rise and fall as history unfolds. Marxism is the inverse of liberalism, in that it replaces the intellectual with the material. The competition of economic classes is also much more intensified than the competition between opinions and commercial interests under liberalism. The Marxist class struggle is violent and bloody. Belief in parliamentary debate is replaced with belief in "direct action". Drawing from the same rationalist intellectual tradition as the radical democrats, Marxism rejects parliamentarianism as a sham covering the dictatorship of a particular class, i.e., the bourgeoisie. True democracy is achieved through the reversal of class relations under a proletarian state that rules in the interest of the laboring majority. Such a state need not utilize formal democratic procedures, but may exist as an "educational dictatorship" that functions to enlighten the proletariat regarding its true class interests. Schmitt then contrasts the rationalism of both liberalism and Marxism with irrationalism. Central to irrationalism is the idea of a political myth, comparable to the religious mythology of previous belief

---

4    Schmitt, *Crisis*, p. 35

systems, and originally developed by the radical left-wing but having since been appropriated by revolutionary nationalists. It is myth that motivates people to action, whether individually or collectively. It matters less whether a particular myth is true than if people are inspired by it.

It is clear enough that Schmitt's criticisms of liberalism are intended not so much as an effort to undermine democratic legitimacy as much as an effort to confront the weaknesses of the intellectual foundations of liberal democracy with candor and intellectual rigor, not necessarily to undermine liberal democracy, but out of recognition of the need for strong and decisive political authority capable of acting in the interests of the nation during perilous times. Schmitt remarks:

> "If democratic identity is taken seriously, then in an emergency no other constitutional institution can withstand the sole criterion of the peoples' will, however it is expressed." [5]

In other words, the state must first act to preserve itself and the general welfare and well-being of the people at large. If necessary, the state may override narrow partisan interests, parliamentary procedure or, presumably, routine electoral processes. Such actions by political leadership may be illiberal, but not necessarily undemocratic, as the democratic general will does not include national suicide. Schmitt outlines this theory of the survival of the state as the first priority of politics in *The Concept of the Political*. The essence of the "political" is the existence of organized collectives prepared to meet existential threats to themselves with lethal force if necessary. The "political" is different from the moral, the aesthetic, the economic or the religious as it involves first and foremost the possibility of groups of human beings killing other human beings. This does not mean that war is necessarily "good" or something to be desired or agitated for.

---

5    *Sourcebook*, p.337

Indeed, it may sometimes be in the political interests of a state to avoid war. However, any state that wishes to survive must be prepared to meet challenges to its existence, whether from conquest or domination by external forces or revolution and chaos from internal forces. Additionally, a state must be capable of recognizing its own interests and assume sole responsibility for doing so. A state that cannot identify its enemies and counter enemy forces effectively is threatened existentially.

Schmitt's political ideas are more easily understood in the context of Weimar's political situation. He is considering the position of a defeated and demoralized Germany; unable to defend itself against external threats, and threatened internally by weak, chaotic and unpopular political leadership, economic hardship, political and ideological polarization and growing revolutionary movements, sometimes exhibiting terrorist or fanatical characteristics. Schmitt regards Germany as desperately in need of some sort of foundation for the establishment of a recognized, legitimate political authority capable of upholding the interests and advancing the well-being of the nation in the face of foreign enemies and above domestic factional interests. This view is far removed from the Nazi ideas of revolution, crude racial determinism, the cult of the leader and war as a value unto itself. Schmitt is clearly a much different thinker than the adherents of the quasi-mystical nationalism common to the radical right-wing of the era. Weimar's failure was due in part to the failure of political leadership to effectively address the questions raised by Schmitt.

# Friedrich Nietzsche

Among the many great and enormously influential thinkers of the nineteenth century, it is Friedrich Wilhelm Nietzsche (1844-1900) who arguably stands the highest in terms of possessing both the most profound and penetrating criticisms of Western civilization as it was in his time, and the most prescient insights and predictions as to what the future course of the evolution of the West would involve. In our own day, Nietzsche has been a popular topic of academic discourse for some time, and the reading of his works has long been a popular pastime among trendy undergraduates. Yet in Nietzsche's day, he remained obscure and his works were not widely read or accepted until after his death. Even with the abundance of Nietzsche scholarship that has been produced in the more than a century since his passing, his core ideas remain widely misunderstood or misinterpreted. Indeed, Nietzsche has been largely appropriated by the academic Left, a great irony considering his own considerable contempt for the politics of the Left, and the prevailing academic philosophy of postmodernism includes the philosophy of Nietzsche as a direct ancestor in its genealogical line.

No thinker is more important or relevant to the ideas of the Conservative Revolution than Nietzsche. While Marx continues to retain his status as the most influential radical thinker of the nineteenth century, it was Nietzsche who was the more revolutionary of the two in the actual implications of his thought. Nietzsche also stands as a polar opposite of the conservative counterrevolutionaries that arose in opposition to the spread of the influence of the Enlightenment. Nietzsche is no mere traditionalist in the vein of Edmund Burke, Joseph De Maistre, or Luis De Bonald. His outlook involves a dramatic departure not only from traditional Western thought as it had unfolded since the time of the Socratics, but from the intellectual culture of even the most advanced or revolutionary thinkers of his own time.

## The Historical Context of Nietzsche's Thought

An adequate understanding of Nietzsche is impossible without recognition of the historical context in which he wrote. Nietzsche's core works were produced between 1872 and 1888. By that time, the intellectual revolution of the Enlightenment was well-established among Western intellectual elites and among the rising educated middle classes. The Enlightenment intellectual revolution and its outgrowths were existential in nature. The most important aspect of the impact of the revolution was what Nietzsche characterized as the "death of God." Advancements in human knowledge in a wide variety of areas had the effect of undermining the credibility of traditional theological views on cosmology, moral philosophy, the meaning of human existence, and so forth. The overthrow of the Christian worldview that had dominated Western civilization for fifteen hundred years left subsequent thinkers with a number of ultimately profound questions.[11] If the purpose of an individual's life is not to achieve salvation in an afterlife, then what is the purpose of life? If the king or established political authorities do not rule by divine right, then what is the basis of political legitimacy? How should society be organized? If morality is not to be understood according to the teachings of the Church, the Bible, or traditional religious authority, then what is the basis of justice, morality, truth or "right and wrong"? Do such concepts have any intrinsic or objective meaning at all? If the observable universe was not the product of special creation by a divine power, and if humanity was not "created in the image of God," then what is the meaning of existence? Does it have any meaning beyond itself? If history

---

1    Peter Gay, *The Enlightenment: The Rise of Modern Paganism* (New York and London: W.W. Norton and Company, 1966), pp. 8-9, 62-63.

is not guided by divine providence, then how is the process of historical unfolding to be understood? These are the questions that Western thinkers have been grappling with since the older, theological view of the universe and existence was demolished by the intellectual innovations of the Enlightenment.

## The New Religion of Reason and Progress

Western civilization existed for millennia prior to the rise of Roman Christianity, so it is unsurprising that anti-Christian, Enlightenment intellectuals found inspiration in the classic works of antiquity. The Enlightenment thinkers (the "*philosophes*") developed a worldview and philosophical outlook relatively similar to that which prevailed among the great thinkers of Greco-Roman intellectual culture.[2] The traditional Christian emphasis on faith, revelation, mystery, and divine authority was rejected in favor of a new emphasis on the efficacy of human reason and ability to engage in rational criticism. The Enlightenment view of the universe mirrored the human-centered outlook of the Greeks, with the ideas of the *philosophes* reflecting the Greek adage that "man is the measure of all things" to a much greater degree than Christian thought had ever done. It was the view of the *philosophes* that human reason and rational thought alone possessed the capability for the discernment of profound insight into the workings of the universe through the use of science. This confidence had been generated by the scientific revolution of the seventeenth century. Human reason was likewise capable of discerning the workings of society and of discovering ways by which society and humanity could be improved upon. Out of this conviction emerged an intellectual optimism that expressed great confidence in the possibility and inevitability of progress. This intellectual framework that was bequeathed to subsequent generations of Europeans by the great thinkers of the Enlightenment formed the foundation for most of modern thought.

---

2    Gay, pp. 59-127.

The concept of progress was a dominant feature of every major aspect of nineteenth century thinking, whether in the areas of philosophy, politics, or science. Thinkers of the German Idealist School, such as Immanuel Kant and G. W. F. Hegel, attempted to retain the notion of justice, morality, and virtue as concepts possessing transcendent characteristics in a manner similar to that found in earlier Christian approaches to moral philosophy. Hegel developed a philosophical doctrine known as "historicism" that characterized the process of human historical development as one by which reason unfolds towards a higher state of rational unity that contains within itself the collection of prior expressions of, and resolved contradictions within, human thought. Hegel gave a metaphysical and quasi-theological gloss to his philosophical system in a way that is still debated and subject to varying interpretations. Yet, this linear, progressive view of history postulated by Hegel established the framework for historical interpretation that would dominate Western thought for the next century.[3]

Karl Marx and Friedrich Engels developed a materialist conception of Hegel's interpretation of history as a dialectical process. The core component of the Marxist interpretation of history is a kind of economic determinism. According to Marxism, history is the manifestation of the struggle between competing socio-economic classes. Other aspects of human life such as politics, religion, culture, family, and philosophy are merely expressions or outgrowths of the material foundations of a given society. Marxism regards history as an evolutionary process whereby class conflict serves as the dialectical process whose impact is the advancement of humanity to a higher stage of social development.[4]

---

3    Georg W.F. Hegel, *The Philosophy of History*, (Amherst, New York: Prometheus Books, 1991).

4    Karl Marx and Friedrich Engels, *The Communist Manifesto* (New York: International Publishers, 1948.)

The nineteenth century idea of progress was further strengthened by the scientific innovations of the time. Evolutionary thinking became dominant in the natural sciences as the older, religious views on the origins of humanity and the universe fell into intellectual disrepute. The prevailing model of evolutionary theory of the era was the "developmental" model. This framework suggested that the evolutionary process was a manifestation of a linear drive towards a particular end. The analogy often used was that of the growth of an individual. The conventional view was that evolution transpires in a way that demonstrates direction and purpose. This particular rendition of evolution, most famously represented by the theories of Jean Baptiste Lamarck, was exploded by Charles Darwin. Darwin argued that evolution takes place through a process of adaption by means of natural selection.[5]

Darwin's actual theory indicated that the process of natural biological evolution exhibits a great deal of randomness, and unfolds in a haphazard way with no specific outcome being inevitable regarding the ends of the evolutionary process. The actual implications of authentic Darwinian evolutionary theory severely detracted from the established "developmental" model of not only biological evolution but also human social evolution.[6] Yet the publication of Darwin's work had the effect of popularizing evolutionary thinking, even if his ideas were misunderstood or misinterpreted. Subsequent thinkers would attempt to find justification for their preferred social or political views in Darwinian evolutionary biology.[7] Marx considered Darwin to have found a scientific justification for his own views on socio-economic evolution, and Darwin was also appropriated by racists and proponents of chauvinistic nationalism. Indeed, efforts to interpret human social evolution within the context of

---

5    Peter J. Bowler, *The Non-Darwinian Revolution: Reinterpreting a Historical Myth.* (Baltimore and London: Johns-Hopkins University Press, 1988), pp. 9-10, 43-44, 24-28, 40-45.

6    Bowler, pp. 9-14.

7    Bowler, pp. 132-158.

a pseudo-Darwinian biological framework became rather open-ended in nature. Proponents of social reform, humanitarians, advocates of predatory capitalism, utopians, racial supremacy theorists, and proponents of class warfare all appealed to Darwin as a justification for their beliefs, all of which were rooted in a fundamental misunderstanding of Darwin's actual ideas.[8] It was the philosophy of Nietzsche that provided the interpretive framework of human history that was the most compatible with the implications of genuine Darwinism.

## The Revolt against Reason and Progress: The Philosophy of Nietzsche

If Darwinian evolutionary biology exploded the nineteenth century idea of progress in the realm of the natural sciences, it was the thought of Nietzsche that provided the most far-reaching assault on the presumptions of the time in the world of philosophy. Nietzsche is perhaps most well-known for his statements concerning the "death of God," but the meaning of the "death of God" in Nietzschean philosophy involves a good deal more than mere conventional atheism. Other prominent intellectual atheists had come before Nietzsche such as Diderot, d'Holbach and (by implication) Hume, and he was by no means the inventor of modern atheism.[9] While Nietzsche was certainly an "anti-theological" thinker in the sense of rejecting a theistic worldview in a conventional religious sense, his notion of the "death of God" was also intended as a critique of the intellectual presumptions of his own era, including those of intellectual elites who had rejected conventional religious faith. While Nietzsche was an atheist, materialist, and rationalist of a kind comparable to the most radical Enlightenment thinkers, his outlook sharply diverges from the Enlightenment tradition with regards to the role of reason in human life and thought.

---

8    Bowler, pp. 166-173.

9    Gay, pp. 63-64, 103, 105, 407-419.

Nietzsche regarded the Enlightenment emphasis on reason as having the effect of denying the role of the passions in forming human character, and shaping human action and human societies. He contrasted the Enlightenment's orientation towards reason with the earlier manifestations and emphasis on the passions he considered to have been made manifest by the Renaissance. He compared these two eras within the framework of his famous Appollonian/Dionysian dichotomy. The Apollonian aspect of human essence is the rational, logical, prudent and restrained. The Dionysian is the instinctual, impulsive, and emotive. Nietzsche was not a skeptic of the passions in the manner of Hobbes or Burke, who regarded human passion and feeling as prone towards dangerous excesses and in need of restraint. Instead, he counseled human beings to live dangerously. Nietzsche regarded the passionate and the irrational (or pre-rational) as the foundation of all high cultures, which he in turn considered to be apex of human existence. The Greeks had emphasized and explored the passions, rather than having feared or shunned them, and for this reason the Greeks had produced the highest of hitherto existing human civilizations. Nietzsche vehemently opposed the rising egalitarian sentiments and trends towards mass society and mass democracy of his era. Only an elite motivated by the passions can produce a high culture. An egalitarian society would be a society of weak and fearful mediocrities concerned only with comfort and safety.

The "death of God" was intended as an attack on philosophical idealism of the kind retained by Kant and Hegel as much as it was an attack on the Christian faith. Nietzsche's philosophy insisted that there is no transcendent or metaphysical foundation for ethics, morality, or justice. Values of this kind are mere human constructions. They have no meaning aside from what human beings, individually or collectively, assign to them. Nietzsche likewise rejected the view of history represented by Hegel's historicism. One of Nietzsche's earliest works, *The Use and Abuse of History*, is an attack on Hegel.[10] The linear view of history contained within Hegel's philosophical system had many precedents in Western thought, with roots going back as least as far as Aristotle. According to Nietzsche, history has no purpose. It is merely a series of events that have no meaning in and of themselves, other than subjective meanings adopted by individuals and human groups relative to their own time, place, and experiences. Nietzsche's philosophy was an attack on virtually the entire legacy of Western metaphysics since the time of Plato.

Nietzsche regarded the nineteenth century idea of progress and the myriad of ideologies, movements, and causes of the time that were a manifestation of this idea to be superstitions every bit as much as the theological superstitions that dominated the Christian era. His parable of the madman found in *The Gay Science* is to be interpreted in this way.[11] Nietzsche is ridiculing the intellectuals of his time who believe they have attained a superior state of enlightenment, and who regard themselves as the progenitors of a higher civilization. He is instead arguing that the thinkers of his time have not yet fully recognized the consequences of the "death of God" for Western civilization. Instead, they are simply trying to find substitutes by replacing old dogmas and pieties with new ones. Among these new gods are socialism, liberalism, utopianism, humanism, nationalism, democracy, pseudo-scientific racism of the kind represented by thinkers such as H.S. Chamberlain[12] and the anti-Semitism of his former friend Richard Wagner. Such efforts are dismissed by Nietzsche as methods of avoiding or postponing the existential crisis that Western civilization would ultimately have to face. Nietzsche attacked even the conservatives of his era for making

---

10   Werner J. Dannhauser, "Friedrich Nietzsche," *History of Political Philosophy*, edited by Joseph Cropsey and Leo Strauss. (Chicago and London: University of Chicago Press, 1963, 1972) Third edition, 1987, pp. 829-831.

11   *Friedrich Nietzsche, A Nietzsche Reader* (London and New York: Penguin Books, 1977), pp. 202-203.

12   *Houston Stewart Chamberlain, Foundations of the Nineteenth Century.* Vol. I. Trans. John Lees. (New York: Howard Fertig, Inc., 1968).

too many concessions to rising egalitarian movements such as democracy and socialism, and for retaining their allegiance to the corpse of Christianity. He dismissed the traditional European aristocracies as weak and in a state of decay, and he also opposed the rising nationalist movements of his time as symptomatic of the egalitarian mass societies of mediocre individuals he saw on the horizon. Nietzsche presciently suggested that the twentieth century would be a time of great wars between the rising ideological mass movements of his own time, and that it would be the twenty-first century before the existential crisis for civilization is fully recognized.

Nietzsche's prophecy that the twentieth century would be a time of war on an unprecedented scale between polarized ideological forces found its realization in the Great War and then the Second World War, and the destructiveness of the latter surpassed even the shocking brutality of the former. The suffering and death generated by the two world wars, and the invention of weapons technology with the capacity to destroy all of mankind demolished the nineteenth century faith in progress and pushed postwar intellectuals towards a confrontation with the nihilistic implications of modern science and philosophy of the kind Nietzsche had previously written about. Existentialism, with its implicitly or explicitly Nietzschean roots, became the prevailing philosophical outlook for intellectuals in the mid to late twentieth century. Existentialism represents an effort to confront the crisis of nihilism suggested by Nietzsche and the serious problems this crisis poses for human ethics and the question of meaning. If existence has no meaning, then what is the basis for proper human behavior? If God is dead, is everything permitted, as Dostoevsky suggested? The struggles of existentialist thinkers with these questions are famously illustrated, for instance, by the efforts of the feminist-existentialist Simone De Beauvoir to establish a framework of ethics in the face of the meaninglessness of existence by pointing to the commonness of the human experience, and the possibility of creating shared virtues and values that advance human interests in the realm of lived experience, even if these values ultimately have no objective or cosmic foundation or meaning.[13] Her companion Jean-Paul Sartre argued that one could create one's own meaning by participating in the social or political activities of one's time or even by embracing the irrational by, for example, becoming a devout Christian or a militant Communist. Sartre himself chose the latter.

## The Future

Nietzsche predicted that it would be well into the twenty-first century before Western thought fully confronted the crisis of nihilism. It would thus far appear that he was correct. Western thought since the Enlightenment has attempted to compensate for the loss of the old faith by replacing the discredited Christian worldview with new faiths and new pieties. As these have become increasingly difficult to justify within a framework of rationality and a belief in inevitable "progress," Western intellectuals have increasingly retreated into the irrational. This is illustrated by the curious phenomena of the present efforts by Western intellectual elites to embrace postmodernism, with its accompanying moral and cultural relativism, while simultaneously embracing the egalitarian-universalist-humanist moralistic zealotry popularly labeled "political correctness" and espousing with great piousness such liberal crusades as "human rights," "anti-racism", "gay liberation," feminism, environmentalism and the like. Such an outlook, which combines extreme moralism in the cultural and political realm, complete moral relativism in the philosophical or metaphysical realm, and at times even falls into subjectivism in the epistemological realm[14], is fundamentally irrational, of course. That such an outlook has become so deeply entrenched indicates that Western intellectuals are desperately working to avoid a full confrontation with the crisis of nihilism.

---

13   Simone De Beauvoir, *The Ethics of Ambiguity*, (Secauscus, New Jersey: Citadel Press, 1948).

14   Michel Foucault, *Madness and Civilization: A History of Insanity in the Age of Reason*, (New York: Vintage Books, 1965), Originally published in 1961.

Pareto argued that civilizations die when their elites lose faith in their own civilization to such a degree that the will to survive no longer exists. Western political and cultural elites presently exhibit abiding contempt for the legacy of their civilization, as demonstrated by their attachment to anti-Western ideologies such as "multiculturalism" and support for political policies, such as permitting mass immigration into the West from the Third World, that ultimately mean the demographic overrun and death of Western civilization.

The presumption of present day elites is that dramatic demographic alteration can transpire without consequences of significance, or that the overthrow of Western civilization itself may even be desirable. The prevalence of such attitudes once again indicates that cultural nihilism has become rather deeply entrenched. Yet this nihilism has been thus far masked by liberal-humanist platitudes of escalating silliness. It remains to be seen what will eventually bring this crisis to the forefront. Genuine threats to the survival of Western civilization itself may well force such a confrontation. These might include the threat of nuclear terrorism, economic collapse or ecological catastrophe, the depletion of resources on which civilization has become dependent, or confrontation with an ideological rival that poses an existential threat. As demographic change on a magnitude that threatens cultural dispossession becomes increasingly imminent, and as the consequences of such become increasingly undeniable, perhaps a belated cultural awakening and renewal will begin. Otherwise, it may well be the case that Western modernity and post-modernity will eventually suffer the same fate as the classical Greco-Roman civilization of antiquity.

# Nietzsche the Visionary

Friedrich Nietzsche suggested in the nineteenth century that the crisis of Western civilization generated by modernity's overthrow of the traditional European order and the loss of faith resulting from the torpedoing of traditional theology by advancements in human knowledge would have repercussions that would endure for two centuries. As the twenty-first century now enters its second decade, the confrontation with that crisis becomes ever more imminent.[15] At present, Western civilization continues to exhibit symptoms of advanced decay and the five hundred year position of Western Europe and its colonial offspring as the dominant centers of power on the earthly stage is steadily being eclipsed by the rise of new great powers represented by such nations as Russia, China, India, and Brazil. Likewise, mass immigration from the Third World into the West threatens to erode the demographic majority of indigenous European peoples in their traditional homelands by the middle to latter part of the century. The egalitarian ethos that provides the foundation of the self-legitimating ideology of the Western ruling classes becomes ever more absurd in its pronouncements and oppressive in its practices with each passing decade.

Future historians will likely look back on the contemporary West as a madhouse where the classic virtues of heroism, high culture, nobility, self-respect, and reason had almost completely disappeared, along with the characteristics of adulthood generally. The present era is the era of the Last Man. The legacy of mass democracy and the values of therapeutic liberalism has been the creation of a culture of infantilism. The morality of *ressentiment* is now the public morality. The guiding principles of contemporary liberal democracies are an all-pervasive consumerism and loudly proclaiming one's own status as an official victim of historic or cosmic injustices, whether real or imaginary. Self-indulgence has been surpassed only by self-pity as the guiding principle of an individual's relationship to the wider society. The commercial values of capitalism, the egalitarian values

---

15    Keith Preston, "The Nietzschean Prophecies: Two Hundred Years of Nihilism and the Coming Crisis of Western Civilization," *The Radical Tradition: Philosophy, Metapolitics & the Conservative Revolution,* edited by Troy Southgate (Primordial Traditions, 2011).

of Marxism, the psychological values of therapeutic culture, and the tendency toward mob rule inherent in mass democracy have been synthesized by modern societies in such a way as to make the wider and more fundamental values related to the preservation and perpetuation of civilization itself virtually impotent. Perhaps even more dreadful has been the exportation of these manifestations of cultural degeneration to nearly every corner of the globe. The Americanization process generated by globalization brings with it a cancer that threatens the survival of ancient cultures that have thus far endured for millennia.

Nietzsche was one of the great visionaries who recognized this process as it was unfolding even in its early stages. In contrast to the notion of progress that dominated so much of nineteenth century thought, Nietzsche regarded much of the history of Western civilization itself as a process of degeneration and decline. The advent of Platonic thought marked a degenerative departure from the time of the pre-Socratics, whom he regarded as representing the peak era of classical civilization. The Christian conquest of the classical world was still further degeneration and, indeed, the time when cultural rot really began to take root. Modernity carried the degenerative process even further to the point where, in the latter part of the nineteenth century, Western civilization had reached the terminal stage. Nietzsche correctly predicted that the twentieth century would be a time of great warfare between mass ideological movements and that this great convulsion of Western civilization would be the prelude to the confrontation with the crisis of nihilism in the twenty-first century.[16]

The most poignant question raised by Nietzsche's philosophy involves the matter of what will emerge on the other side of Western civilization's historical trajectory once modernity and post-modernity have finally expired. It would appear that there are two primary routes which the unfolding of Western history may take. One of these is the extinction of Western civilization

16   *Ibid.*

itself resulting from the combined forces of a loss of international power, internal rot, and demographic overrun. The other would be some sort of cultural renewal and awakening. It is this latter option for which the vision of Nietzsche provides inspiration. What would a future post-postmodern Western civilization actually look like? What would be its guiding values, mores, social structures, and political institutions? Nietzsche himself was rather vague on what his ideal type of society might be. So Nietzsche's own preferences or inclinations regarding such questions have to be inferred rather than directly discerned.

It is clear enough that Nietzsche was not and would not today be any kind of conventional "conservative." Indeed, Nietzsche had little regard for the conservatives of even his own time. He regarded the European nobility as decadent and unwilling to fight to retain its historic and traditional place when confronted with the rising egalitarian movements of the era. His admonition that men should aspire to greater cruelty is to be interpreted in light of his criticisms of the weakness of the noble classes. Nietzsche was a firm believer in Pareto's later axiom that he who becomes a lamb will be devoured by the wolves. He presciently saw that the European elite lacked the resolve to effectively counter the dangers posed by the growing ideological extremisms of the era. Nietzsche was the anti-Marx. He held even the conservative icon Bismarck in contempt for his embrace of egalitarian measures like universal suffrage and extensive welfare state legislation. Nietzsche also disdained the embrace of nationalism by modern conservatives and opposed Bismarck's project of unification of Germany's previously sovereign regions under a centralized national regime. Instead, Nietzsche considered nationalism to be a manifestation of the same egalitarian tendencies of mass society as movements like socialism and communism.[17]

17   Werner J. Dannhauser, "Friedrich Nietzsche," *History of Political Philosophy*, edited by Joseph Cropsey and Leo Strauss. Chicago and London: University of Chicago Press, 1963, 1972, Third edition, 1987, pp. 829-831.

Contrary to the popular vulgarized interpretation of Nietzsche's thought as a forerunner to Fascism and National Socialism, Nietzsche was greatly alarmed by the growth of the modern state and of the tendency towards militarism resulting from the mass armies made possible by the modern state's powers of conscription. The form of the state that began to emerge in the nineteenth century exemplified Hobbes' characterization of the absolute ruler as an all-encompassing Leviathan. The massive growth of the state was the end result of the growth of mass political participation through democratic suffrage and of mass political movements reflecting popular ideological enthusiasm. This was a criticism of the modern state that would be revisited by twentieth century elite theorists such as Jose Ortega y Gasset. As Michael Kleen has observed:

> The State was a temple in which the masses worshipped themselves. In exchange for catering to their needs and flattering their egos, the masses placed their collective will under the auspices of the State where they flourished like never before in history. For both Nietzsche and Ortega, that arrangement was Janus-faced, because although the masses grew in ever-increasing numbers— high art, music, education, and individualism in general suffered. European culture began to decay. Violence and militarism (especially of the uniform variety) became the order of the day.[18]

Clearly, a society which reflected Nietzschean ideals would roll back the growth of the modern Leviathan state and would eschew the national chauvinisms and aggressive militarism which characterized much of right-wing and left-wing politics alike during the twentieth century. In his own predictably unique way, Nietzsche might be said to have embraced a kind of pan-European cosmopolitanism. Says Michael Kleen:

---

18    Michael Kleen, "Nietzsche and Ortega Juxtaposed," *Strike-the-Root.Com*, August 18, 2010. Archived at http://www.strike-the-root.com/nietzsche-and-ortega-juxtaposed

Unfortunately, Nietzsche did not leave a well thought out alternative to the modern state. Instead, he left his readers to infer his preference based on the political arrangements he criticized. In *Human, All-Too Human* (1878), however, he touched on nationalism and the nation state, proposing that it would be a benefit to Europeans to abolish nations and breed a "European man" that would contain the best qualities of all peoples living on the continent. He envisioned a noble class that freely exchanged ideas across Europe. Based on his other arguments, we can surmise that Nietzsche was *not* advocating something along the lines of a European Union or a transnational state, but perhaps a collection of thousands of municipalities along the lines of the ancient Greek *polis*.[19]

This inference regarding what Nietzsche's preferred political model might have been, seems apt enough given his suggestion that pre-Socratic classical civilization constituted the apex of Western cultural achievement.

Given Nietzsche's pronounced hostility to the state, it is interesting to note his disdain for the anarchist movements of his era. He apparently regarded these as secularized versions of Christian utopian other-worldliness.[20] This is a fair criticism given the strident millenarian strands to be found within classical anarchism, the influence of Rousseau-inspired egalitarianism on classical anarchist thought, and the embrace of anarchism by Christian moralists like Tolstoy. Nietzsche might be said to be a manifestation of a non-egalitarian anarchism, or an "anarchism of the Right," just as he is more widely known as an exponent of "atheism of the Right" with his strident critique of Christian slave-morality. It is also doubtful that Nietzsche would be particularly enamored of modern libertarian thought, with its roots in classical liberalism, its embrace of Enlightenment rationalism, and its

19    Michael Kleen, "Nietzsche and the State," *Strike-the-Root.Com*, July 15, 2010. Archived at http://www.strike-the-root.com/nietzsche-and-state

20    Charles Bufe, "Introduction," The Philosophy of Friedrich Nietzsche, by Henry Louis Mencken. San Francisco: See Sharp Press. Originally published in 1908.

vulgar reduction of social life to that of *homo economicus*. The rise of the classical bourgeoisie in the eighteenth and nineteenth centuries was accompanied by all of the social and political trends that Nietzsche detested: mass democracy, the centralized nation-state, imperialism, and massive national armies. If he regarded the hereditary European nobility as decrepit, he would have regarded the rising bourgeoisie upper middle class as even more degenerate than the aristocracy it aimed to replace. If the Christian foundations of the *ancient regime* represented a deterioration of classical civilization to Nietzsche, how much more deplorable would he have found the *economism* of the bourgeoisie.

Indeed, Nietzsche's contrast of the Appollonian and the Dionysian foreshadows the latter critique of the rationalization of modern life advanced by Weber. For Nietzsche, rationality leaves no space for the passions. Though his own atheism and materialism were clearly derivative of latter Enlightenment thought, Nietzsche himself was an admirer of the Renaissance, not the Enlightenment. One can only imagine the contempt Nietzsche would have for contemporary Western societies and their institutionalization of the morality of *ressentiment* and their preoccupation with safety and security. As Nietzsche counseled men to live dangerously, he would no doubt regard, for instance, the present trend towards redefining long established childhood games and toys as menacing hazards or ordinary foods as the near-equivalent of poisons as an affront to authentic virtue. He would no doubt regard the now all-pervasive institutionalization of what has been termed "political correctness" to be the ultimate in the elevation of slave-morality and the inversion of nobility. Nietzsche would likely regard contemporary therapeutic culture as a form of human degeneration that even he might have been previously inclined to regard as impossible. He would no doubt observe the circus-like atmosphere of contemporary American politics and wonder, "How can this be?" If he were a contemporary man, Nietzsche might well observe the present state of Western culture and repeat the words of Christ at Gethsamane: *"Let this cup pass from me!"*

A Nietzschean civilization would be one where men were once again not only invited but encouraged to live dangerously. Clearly, such a society would be an aristocracy, but not just any kind of aristocracy. It is doubtful that Nietzsche would have seriously regarded the hereditary nobility as a manifestation of his own ideal. An authentically Nietzschean aristocracy would certainly maintain more stringent requirements for admission than mere accident of birth. A Nietzschean aristocracy would therefore be an aristocracy of merit rather than inheritance, but it would not be the pseudo-aristocracy of the bourgeoisie elites for whom prowess at money-making represents the highest human type. Nor would it be the New Class bureaucratic elite that emerged in the twentieth century and from which much of the contemporary upper middle class is drawn.[21] It is this class that is at present challenging the domination of the traditional bourgeoisie.[22] Nietzsche would have certainly regarded the New Class as even more degenerative than the bourgeoisie itself. Nor would the aristocracy of merit be comprised of a set of totalitarian dictators of the kind normally identified with Fascism, Communism, or National Socialism. The political institutions of a prototypical Nietzschean society would be neither feudal nor capitalist nor social democratic nor totalitarian.

It is clear that in such a society economic values would play a secondary role to cultural and aristocratic values. The commercial class and the political class would not be allowed to merge in the way that they have in modern bourgeoisie societies. As Nietzsche advocated a frank atheism, it also obvious that religious institutions would likewise play a secondary role and remain separated from the state in the same manner as contemporary liberal societies. This does not necessarily mean that society as a whole would espouse atheism. Atheism may well retain its present

---

21   Alvin W. Gouldner, *The Future of Intellectuals and the Rise of the New Class*. New York: Continuum Publishing Service, 1979.

22   Scott Locklin, "Social Classes: The Upper Middle Class," *AlternativeRight.Com*, August 17, 2010. Archived at http://www.alternativeright.com/main/blogs/zeitgeist/social-classes-the-upper-middle-class/

status as the dominant perspective of intellectual elites with the common people and a minority of elites practicing the religion most compatible with their own cultural identity and familial ancestry. The renewed interest in recent times among Western peoples in primordial faiths and the growth of various forms of paganism may be an indication of a revival of non-Christian traditional Western faiths in the future. Christianity may well have to share space on the cultural stage with Odinism or Asatru at some point in the future just as it now increasingly has to share space with Wicca, Islam, Eastern mysticism, Deism, the myriad of "New Age" sects, and so forth. Tradition would certainly be an important aspect of a society organized as an aristocracy of merit, but tradition would not be an end unto itself. Nietzsche was, after all, a revolutionary whose thinking was more radical in its implications than even the thought of Marx. Tradition in a civilization guided by the ideals of Nietzsche would be regarded as a continuum that connects the present with the past and which regards the present as a bridge from the past to the future. Tradition would likewise be considered as a force which provides the individual with a sense of place within the context of these wider historical forces. Yet such a reverence for tradition would not imply stasis. Tradition would be regarded as pathway in an ongoing journey and not a final endpoint.

The most compelling question that arises from speculation on the nature of a Nietzschean society is the one that considers from where a revolutionary aristocracy would arise. Just as an aristocracy of this kind would not be one whose claim to merit was rooted in mere financial acumen, so would such an aristocracy necessarily be more than a band of political opportunists who happened to seize power through guile, connivance, and manipulation. Though Nietzsche advised men to increase their cruelty, it does not necessarily follow that a Nietzschean aristocracy would be devoid of the traditional principle of *noblesse oblige*. The Nietzschean elites are not tyrants. The demise of institutions which Nietzsche abhorred such as mass democracy, the modern state, the domination of commercial interests, decrepit religious denominations, and mass armies would no doubt strengthen other institutions, including many that are at present being smothered by the forces of modernity. The most obvious among these are the family, tribe, clan, and community. Still others are guilds, fraternities, cultural organizations, educational institutions that exist independently of the wider political apparatus of mass democracy, philanthropies, localized associations for the pursuit of community activities, law, science, art, athletics, professions, labor associations, farmers association, citizen posses, regional militias, and many more possible examples. Within each of these kinds of human social arrangements, there would likely arise an elite comprised of individuals of superior ability and virtue who came to be regarded by the larger community specifically and the wider society generally as deserving of their position due to their greater merit. Perhaps areas of social life requiring highly specialized levels of expertise would be governed by appointees from scholarly institutions devoted to learning and the cultivation of virtue and wisdom on the part of their individual devotees. Erik von Kuehnelt-Leddihn was fond of pointing to the traditional Chinese civil service examination system as one reflecting the ideals of meritocracy. The scholars who comprised the Mandarin class were drawn from the ranks of those demonstrating superior skill and ability. This was not a hereditary class but one where even the lowliest peasants with remarkable talents could achieve self-advancement.

Indeed, Kuehnelt-Leddihn observed that one of the weaknesses of the Right was its failure to offer a utopia of its own as a counter to the utopias proposed by the Left.[23] It is in the thought of Nietzsche that a very generalized blueprint for the intellectual backdrop of a "Utopia of the Right" can be found. With the emergence of contemporary ideologies like National-Anarchism, a glimpse becomes available into what the future of civilization might be once the era of the Last Man has passed. As one anonymous commentator has suggested:

---

23    Erik von Kuehnelt-Leddihn, *Leftism Revisited: From De Sade and Marx to Hitler and Pol Pot*. Washington, D.C.: Regnery Gateway, 1990.

I think that the future will be a world of dizzying social complexity, replete with small city-states with governments ranging the gamut from democratic to monarchical to theocratic, surrounded by vast hinterlands filled with eco-villages and wild ranges where hunter gatherer humans chase wild game and forage for nuts and berries, while vast trade fleets of ultra-light zeppelins transfer goods and services all over the planet, and transhumanist consciousnesses zip through endless, decentralized computer networks maintained by industrial syndicates a million workers strong, who build satellites and launch them into orbit to maintain a global network of communication so primitivists can use cell-phones to trade furs for plastic-composite bows... and so on.[24]

The decline of existentialism and postmodernism may well represent the final breath of Western philosophy and the fulfillment of Nietzsche's prophecy of the 21st century as the time when Western civilization would have to face the crisis of nihilism. This dissolution of Western philosophy corresponds with the dissolution of Western civilization itself.[25] The pronounced decadence of present day Western elites who actively seek to undermine and destroy their own civilization is the manifestation of the suicidal nihilism of the Last Man. The seemingly inevitable demographic transformation of the West over the next century may well mark the dawn of a new "post-Western West" out of which new primordial myths will arise.

---

24 Chris George, "Wisdom and Vision," *New Kind of Mind*, April 11, 2011. Archived at http://www.newkindofmind.com/2011/04/wisdom-and-vision.html

25 I am grateful to Michael Parish for this insight.

# Hilaire Belloc

## The Servile State and the Political Economy of Distributism

From the beginnings of the Industrial Revolution in the late eighteenth and early nineteenth century until the era of the Great Depression immediately preceding the commencement of the Second World War, the most enduring internal conflict within the nations of the West was rooted in what was then called the "social question." The growth of industrialization and the dispossession of the agrarian peasant classes during the time of the enclosure movement had created within the industrializing nations a massive proletarian class of permanently pauperized laborers and the deplorable social conditions which accompanied the growth of this class.

Throughout the nineteenth century, numerous potential remedies to the condition of the working classes were proposed and the labor, socialist, communist, and anarchist movements developed into powerful political forces during this time. It was into this political and socioeconomic environment that Hilaire Belloc was born in 1870. Belloc was born in France to an English mother and French father and was raised in England. Throughout his eighty-two years of life, Belloc would exhibit many talents. He was an immensely prolific writer (it was once said that he "wrote a library" during his time), poet, and debater. He was an accomplished historian. Belloc was fond of racing yachts and wrote extensively on travel. He was also a politician at one point in his life and for a time held a seat in the English parliament. From his experience as a parliamentarian, Belloc came to regard the pretenses of the liberal democratic state as one rooted in the popular representation of the people as a sham. Parliamentary democracy, in Belloc's view, was simply a mask for the rule of the plutocratic class. Perhaps above all, Belloc was a staunch defender of Catholic orthodoxy and produced many apologetic works on behalf of his own faith tradition and challenged the secularism of his intellectual contemporaries such as George Bernard Shaw and H. G. Wells.[1]

Though Belloc opposed the secular outlook of the Fabian intellectuals and the more radical Marxists, he shared their concern with solving the problems of labor and the social ills brought about by the industrial age. It was out of this concern that Belloc and his friend, fellow literary figure, and fellow Catholic apologist Gilbert Keith Chesterton formed a unique and always small but intellectually original movement known as "distributism." The philosophical basis of distributism was outlined in two books, one by Chesterton and one by Belloc. Chesterton's *What's Wrong with the World* was published in 1910. Its thesis was that the paternalistic welfare state proposed by the progressive liberal and social democratic reformers of the era was not inconsistent with the continued rule of the plutocrats. Rather, a welfare state of the kind the Fabians suggested could be utilized by the ruling classes to pacify and further subordinate the working classes. Belloc continued with this theme in his 1912 book *The Servile State*. Belloc generally accepted the criticisms of capitalism offered by the socialists and Marxists, but argued that socialism would not have the effect of liberating the working classes. Instead, the welfare state would reduce the workers and the masses generally to the level of state dependents with the state continuing to be controlled by the capitalist plutocracy.

As devout Catholic traditionalists, both Belloc and Chesterton naturally had the tendency to romanticize the social system of the medieval era, centered as it was in the Catholic Church. The guilds and agrarian peasant traditions of the Middle Ages

---

1    Jahn, Karl (2000). "Distributism." Archived at http://karljahn.tripod.com/tan/distributism.htm. Accessed on October 8, 2012.

became the model for Belloc's and Chesterton's and by extension the distributist movement's theoretical foundations for social reform. The ambition of the distributists was not to nationalize the means of productions in the manner favored by the Marxists or to radically expand the level of state intervention into the economy and into society in the name of social welfare. Rather, the distributists preferred the opposite approach of redistributing the means of production into as many hands as possible, essentially making everyone into a capitalist. Distributist ideas continued to be outlined in Chesterton's paper *G. K.'s Weekly* and the Distributist League were founded in 1926. Most of the core members of the league were either former socialists who had converted to Catholicism or devout Catholics who were simply concerned with the social question. The league was never a particularly large organization and never held more than two thousand actual members at any one time. Distributism was an intellectual movement rather than a political or activist one.

Distributism is a concept that is more interesting for its ideas than its influence. It was a tendency that offered an uncompromising critique of capitalism yet firmly rejected virtually all efforts or proposals to remedy the ills of capitalism through bureaucracy and statism. Not only the socialist parties but also the labor unions were criticized by the distributists on these grounds. Belloc, Chesterton, and the distributists shared the concern of classical liberals for the preservation of private property and the liberty of the individual against the state while simultaneously expressing concern for the conditions of labor and related social injustices. Capitalism in their view had the effect of a net reduction in liberty not only because the laboring masses were dependent on the capitalists for their subsistence, but also because capitalism was inherently unstable and therefore necessitated state intervention in order to address its social dislocations. Further, the capitalists and plutocrats themselves preferred state regulation of the kind granting monopoly privileges. Contrary to the supposed *laissez faire* ideal of capitalism, the actual practice of capitalism went hand in hand with the growth of statism.

The distributists' criticisms of capitalism were not merely economic in nature. In their view, both capitalism and the proposed socialist alternatives were equally deficient in their neglect of the spiritual welfare of mankind and their limitation of social concerns to matters of material interests only. For the capitalists, greed and material acquisition had become the highest values. For the socialists, satisfying the material needs of the working classes was their only concern. Neither perspective satisfactorily addressed the dehumanizing nature of either proletarianism as it existed under capitalism or the proposed statist alternatives offered by the socialists. The distributists were concerned about the effect of capitalism on family, cultural, and communal life. By forcing the workmen to spend long hours laboring in factories, capitalism was essentially taking fathers and husbands away from their families and the distributists noted that the plutocratic classes would at times endorse women's emancipation movements in order to make female labor more readily exploitable. The concerns of many traditionalists of the era regarding the impact of industrialization and commercial society on high culture were also shared by the distributists and the distributists likewise lamented the decline of small shops and independent craftsmen brought on by the rise of department stores and chain stores.

Though they were critical of the dehumanizing effects of the machine age, the distributists were not advocates of a return to a pre-industrial state in the manner advocated by the Luddites. Rather, they thought that with a widespread distribution of ownership of productive property, the laboring classes would be able to achieve autonomy and independence through such arrangements as industrial guilds operated as cooperatives of small producers and the reestablishment and growth of small businesses and small farms. Indeed, the economic ideals of the distributists were very similar to those of the classical anarchists and both movements favored many similar economic arrangements such as worker cooperatives, mutual banks, and independent peasant communities. The American social reformer and devout Catholic Dorothy Day even attempted a synthesis of distributist and anarchist ideas with her Catholic Worker movement. Yet the Catholic traditionalists and romantic medievalists who comprised the distributist movement generally found themselves at odds with the anarchists and their anti-clericalism and Enlightenment rationalism. However, the differences were primarily philosophical, cultural, and religious rather than economic.[2]

Belloc advanced an interesting theory concerning the development of capitalism in England and by extension throughout the world during the Industrial Revolution. He argued that capitalism took the particular form that it assumed during its developmental era largely as a consequence of the dissolution of the monasteries by Henry VIII during the sixteenth century. The monasteries had previously been the basis of cultural, educational, and charitable life in England and their suppression had created a gap in the social fabric whose consequences were made manifest during the early industrial age. First, the disappearance of the monasteries had the effect of removing the social safety net and creating the conditions for state assumption of charitable responsibilities in the way first demonstrated by the Poor Laws and which later found their full fruition in the welfare state. Likewise, the decline in the power and influence of the Church that was the natural result of the closure of the monasteries undermined the ability of the Church to serve as a constraining force on the growing power of industrial capitalists. Lastly, the destruction of monastic life had the effect of creating a spiritual vacuum that would later be filled by the materialistic values of the growing commercial society.[3]

George Orwell noted in 1946 that Belloc's *The Servile State* had been quite prescient in its analysis of the likely consequences of

---

2    Dorothy Day. "Articles on Distributism-2." *The Catholic Worker,* July–August 1948, 1, 2, 6.

3    Bradshaw, Brendan (1974). *The Dissolution of the Religious Orders in Ireland under Henry VIII.* London: Cambridge University Press.

state socialism when it was published thirty-four year earlier.[4] The legacy of state socialism has been the creation of the hard totalitarian regimes associated with Communism, Fascism, and Nazism, and the soft totalitarianism of the Western welfare states. Belloc has since been demonstrated to have been correct when he suggested that socialism would only have the effect of maintaining plutocratic rule while pacifying the population at large by making them into wards of the provider state. Though living standards have certainly risen in the West since Belloc's time, all of the modern nations now face severe fiscal crises generated in large part by the prevalence of the provider state. The rise of the global economy has brought with it the advance of proletarianism in previously pre-industrial societies on the periphery and generated a process of re-proletarianization in the nations where industrialization is long established, particularly in the United States. The massive transnational capitalist enterprises and financial institutions are now eclipsing the power of even nation-states themselves. In some ways, it would seem that the problems that Belloc and his distributist colleagues sought to address are now as prevalent as ever.

---

4    George Orwell. "Second Thoughts on James Burnham" in *Polemic* No 3 May 1946.

# G. K. Chesterton

## Neither Progressive nor Conservative: The Anti-Modernism of G. K. Chesterton

Gilbert Keith Chesterton (1874-1936) bears the distinction of being a writer who resisted virtually all of the dominant trends of his era. He lived during the late nineteenth and early twentieth century, precisely the time that modernity was fully consolidating itself within Western civilization more than a century after the apex of the Enlightenment and the French Revolution. Chesterton began his writing career as a young man and as the twentieth century was just beginning. As much as any other writer from his era, he predicted the horrors that century would entail.

A man of many talents and interests, Chesterton was a playwright, novelist, lecturer, journalist, poet, critic of literature and art, philosopher, and theologian. His work in many of these areas stands out as being among the very best of the era and continues to offer immense insight even in the present day. Among Chesterton's circle of friends and intellectual sparring partners were such luminaries as H. G. Wells, Bertrand Russell, and George Bernard Shaw. His relationships with these men are themselves highly significant as each of them were among the leading "progressive" intellectuals of the era and fully committed to the modernist values of rationalism, secularism, and socialism. As these were all systems of thought that Chesterton adamantly opposed, it is striking that he could also count some of these figures as friends and engage them in amiable debate. It was during an era when the old liberal values of rational discourse and gentlemanly civility still prevailed, even among those who in many ways held polar opposite world views. It was before the time of the radical political polarization of modern intellectual life that began with the growth of the totalitarian movements of the early to middle twentieth century. The friendly exchanges between Chesterton and Shaw, for instance, even on topics of intense disagreement in many ways serve as a refreshing contrast to the rhetorical brutality that dominates much of today's public discourse.

The dramatic changes that had occurred in Western society over the course of the nineteenth century had dramatically impacted the thinking of its leading intellects. The growth of industrial civilization has raised the general standards of living to levels that were hitherto not even dreamed of, and the rising incomes of the traditionally exploited industrial working class were finally allowing even the proletariat to share in at least some middle class comforts. The rise of new political ideologies such as liberalism and democracy had imparted to ordinary people political and legal rights that were previously reserved only for the nobility. Health standards also increased significantly as industrial civilization expanded and life expectancy began to grow longer. Scientific discovery and technological innovation exploded during the same era and human beings began to marvel at what they had accomplished and might be able to accomplish in the future. Religion-driven superstitions had begun to wane and the religious persecutions of the past had dwindled to near non-existence. Societies became ever more complex and out of this complexity came the need for an ever expanding class of specialists and more scientific approaches to social management. While only a hundred years had passed between the world as it was in 1800 and the world of 1900, the changes that had occurred in the previous century were so profound that the time difference might as well have been thousands of years.

The profundity of this civilization-wide change inspired the leading thinkers of the era to tremendous confidence and optimism regarding the future and human capabilities.

If one surveys the literature of utopian writers of the era one immediately observes that many of these authors expressed a confidence in the future that now seems as quaint as it is absurd. The horrors of the twentieth century, with its genocides, total wars, atomic weaponry, and unprecedented levels of tyranny would subsequently shatter the naïve idealism of many who had previously viewed the advent of that century with great hopes that often approached the fantastic. The early twentieth century was a time of joyous naiveté. Bertrand Russell would later insist that no one who was born after the beginning of the Great War which broke out in 1914 would ever know what it was like to be truly happy.

But G. K. Chesterton, while far from being a cynical or overly pessimistic figure, was not one who shared in this optimism. Indeed, he was one who understood the potential horrors that could be unleashed by the new society and new modes of thought as clearly as any other. To Chesterton, the progressives of his time were over confident to the point of arrogance and failed to recognize the dangers that might befall mankind as humanity boldly forged its way into the future. Perhaps one of Chesterton's most prescient works of social criticism is "Eugenics and Other Evils," published in 1917.[1] At the time the eugenics movement that was largely traceable to the thought of Darwin's cousin, Francis Galton, had become a popular one in the world's most advanced nations such as England, America, and Germany. It was a movement that in its day was regarded as progressive, enlightened and as applying scientific principles to the betterment of human society and even the human species itself. Its supporters included many leading thinkers and public figures of the era including Winston Churchill, Sidney and Beatrice Webb, John Maynard Keynes, Anthony Ludovici, Madison Grant, and Chesterton's friends Wells and Shaw. Yet Chesterton was one of the earliest critics of the eugenics movement and regarded

---

1    Chesterton, Gilbert Keith. *Eugenics and Other Evils*. Reprinted by CreateSpace Independent Publishing Platform; 1st edition (November 20, 2012). Originally published in 1917.

it as representing dangerous presumptions on the part of its proponents that would likely lead to horrific abuses of liberty and violations of the individual person which it eventually did.

One of Chesterton's most persistent targets was the growing secularism of his era, a trend which continues to the present time. That Chesterton was a man of profound faith even as religion was being dwarfed by science among thinking and educated people during his time solidifies Chesterton's role as a true intellectual maverick. It is this aspect of Chesterton's thought that as much as anything else continues to win him the admiration of those who remain believers even during the twenty-first century. Chesterton was always a man of spiritual interests and even as a young man toyed with occultism and Ouija boards. The development of his spiritual thinking later led him to regard himself and an "orthodox" Christian and Chesterton formally converted to Catholicism in 1922 at the age of forty-six. His admirer C. S. Lewis considered Chesterton's writings on Christian subjects to be among the very best works in Christian apologetics.

In the intellectual climate of the early twenty-first century, religious thinking has fallen into even greater disrepute than it possessed in the early twentieth century. In relatively recent times, popular culture has produced a number of writers whose open contempt for religious believers has earned them a great deal of prominence. While intelligent believers who can offer thoughtful defenses of their views certainly still exist, it is also that case that religious belief or practice is at its lowest point yet in terms of popular enthusiasm in the Western world. Less than five percent of the British population attends religious services regularly and even in the United States, with its comparatively large population of religious fundamentalists, secularism has become the fastest growing religious perspective. Chesterton would no doubt be regarded as a rather anachronistic figure in such a cultural climate.

The contemporary liberal and left-wing stereotype of a religious believer is that of an ignorant or narrow-minded bigot who is incapable of flexibility in his thinking and reacts with intolerance to those holding different points of view. Certainly, there are plenty of religious people who fit such stereotypes just as overly rigid and dogmatic persons can be found among adherents of any system of thought. Yet, a survey of both Chesterton's writings on religion and his correspondence with friends of a secular persuasion indicates that Chesterton was the polar opposite of a bigoted, intolerant, religious fanatic. In his Christian apologetic work *Orthodoxy*, Chesterton wrote, "To hope for all souls is imperative, and it is quite tenable that their salvation is inevitable. . .In Christian morals, in short, it is wicked to call a man 'damned': but it is strictly religious and philosophic to call him damnable." Of his friend Shaw, he said, "In a sweeter and more solid civilization he would have been a great saint."

In his later years when he knew he was dying, H. G. Wells wrote to Chesterton, "If after all my Atheology turns out wrong and your Theology right I feel I shall always be able to pass into Heaven (if I want to) as a friend of G.K.C.'s. Bless you." Chesterton wrote in response: "If I turn out to be right, you will triumph, not by being a friend of mine, but by being a friend of Man, by having done a thousand things for men like me in every way from imagination to criticism. The thought of the vast variety of that work, and how it ranges from towering visions to tiny pricks of humor, overwhelmed me suddenly in retrospect; and I felt we have none of us ever said enough. . .Yours always, G. K. Chesterton."[2]

It was also during Chesterton's era that the classical socialist movement was initially starting to become powerful through the trade unions and labor parties and virtually all leading intellectuals of the era professed fidelity to the ideals of socialism. Yet just as Chesterton was prescient critic of eugenics, he

---

2    Babinski, Edward T. "Chesterton and Univeralism." Archived at http://www.tentmaker. org/biographies/chesterton.htm. Accessed on March 12, 2013.

likewise offered an equally prescient critique of the totalitarian implications of state socialism. Because of this, he was often labeled a reactionary or conservative apologist for the plutocratic overlords of industrial capitalism by the Marxists of his era. But Chesterton was no friend of those who would exploit the poor and workings classes and was in fact a staunch critic of the industrial system as it was in the England of his era. *"Who except a devil from Hell ever defended it?"* he was alleged to have said when asked about capitalism as it was practiced in his day.[3]

Indeed, Chesterton's criticisms of both industrial capitalism and state socialism led to the development of one of the most well-known and interesting aspects of his thought, the unique economic philosophy of distributism. Along with his dear friend and fellow Catholic traditionalist Hilaire Belloc (Shaw coined the term "Chesterbelloc" to describe the pair as inseparable as they were), Chesterton suggested the creation of an economic system where productive property would be spread to as many owners of capital as possible thereby producing many "small capitalists" rather than having capital concentrated into the hands of a few plutocrats, trusts, or the state itself. The prevailing trends of the twentieth century were towards ever greater concentrations of power in large scale, pyramid-like institutions and ever expanding bureaucratic profligacy. Chesterton's and Belloc's economic ideas were frequently dismissed as quaint and archaic. However, technological developments in the cyber age have once again opened the door for exciting new possibilities concerning the prospects for the decentralization of economic life. Far from being anachronistic reactionaries, perhaps Chesterton and his friend Belloc were instead futuristic visionaries far ahead of their time.

It is clear enough that Chesterton was in many ways a model for what a public intellectual should be. He was a fiercely

---

3    Friedman, David D. "G. K. Chesterton-An Author Review," *The Machinery of Freedom: Guide to Radical Capitalism.* Second Edition. Archived at http://daviddfriedman.com/The_Machinery_of_Freedom_.pdf. Accessed on March 12, 2013.

and genuinely independent thinker and one who stuck to his convictions with courage. Chesterton never hesitated to buck the prevailing trends of his day and was not concerned about earning the opprobrium of the chattering classes by doing so. He was above all a man of character, committed to intellectual integrity, sincere in his convictions, tolerant in his religious faith, and charitable in his relations with others. In his intellectual life, he wisely and quixotically criticized the worst excesses of the intellectual culture of his time. The twentieth century might have been a happier time if the counsel of G. K. Chesterton had been heeded.

# Julius Evola

## The Sexual Aesthetics and Metaphysics of Julius Evola

Of the various manifestations of the egalitarian cultural revolution that has transpired in the Western world over the past half century, none have been quite so enduring or become so deeply rooted in the culture of modern society as the so-called "sexual revolution." Indeed, it might well be argued that even the supposed commitment of Western cultural elites in the early twenty-first century to the ethos of racial egalitarianism is not quite as profound as their commitment to the preservation and expansion of the victories of the sexual revolution. The sexual revolution itself brings with it many of its own manifestations. These include the now prevailing feminist ethos, the liberalization of both popular opinion and public legislation concerning sexual conduct, abortion and contraception, divorce, the normalization of homosexuality accompanied by the growth of powerful homosexual political interest groups, and the identification of an ever-growing list of "gender identity" or "sexual orientation" groups who are subsequently assigned their position in the Left's pantheon of the oppressed.

Of course, the ongoing institutionalization of the values of the sexual revolution is not without its fierce critics. Predictably, the most strident criticism of sexual liberalism originates from the clerical and political representatives of the institutions of organized Christianity and from concerned Christian laypeople. Public battles over sexual issues are depicted in the establishment media as conflicts between progressive-minded, intelligent and educated liberals versus ignorant, bigoted, sex-phobic reactionaries. Dissident conservative media outlets portray conflicts of this type as pitting hedonistic, amoral sexual libertines against beleaguered upholders of the values of faith, family, and chastity. Yet this "culture war" between liberal libertines and Christian puritans is not what should be the greatest concern of those holding a radical traditionalist or conservative revolutionary outlook.

## Sexuality and the Pagan Heritage of Western Civilization

The European New Right has emerged as the most intellectually progressive and sophisticated contemporary manifestation of the values of the conservative revolution. Likewise, the overlapping schools of thought associated with the ENR have offered the most penetrating and comprehensive critique of the domination of contemporary cultural and political life by the values of liberalism and the consequences of this for Western civilization. The ENR departs sharply from conventional "conservative" criticisms of liberalism of the kind that stem from Christian piety. Unlike the Christian conservatives, the European New Right does not hesitate to embrace the primordial pagan heritage of the Indo-European ancestors of Western peoples. The history of the West is much older than the fifteen hundred year reign of the Christian church that characterized Western civilization from the late Roman era to the early modern period. This history includes foremost of all the classical Greco-Roman civilization of antiquity and its legacy of classical pagan scholarship and cultural life. Recognition of this legacy includes a willingness to recognize and explore classical pagan attitudes towards sexuality. As Mark Wegierski has written:

> The ENR's "paganism" entails naturalism towards mores and sexuality. Unlike still traditionalists, ENR members have a relatively liberated attitude towards sexuality...ENR members have no desire to impose what they consider the patently unnatural moralism of Judeo-Christianity on

sexual relations. However, while relatively more tolerant in principle, they still value strong family life, fecundity, and marriage or relations within one's own ethnic group. (Their objection to intraethnic liaisons would be that the mixture of ethnic groups diminishes a sense of identity. In a world where every marriage was mixed, cultural identity would disappear). They also criticize Anglo-American moralism and its apparent hypocrisy: " . . . In this, they are closer to a worldly Europe than to a puritanical America obsessed with violence. According to the ENR: "Our ancestral Indo-European culture . . . seems to have enjoyed a healthy natural attitude to processes and parts of the body concerned with the bringing forth of new life, the celebration of pair-bonding love, and the perpetuation of the race."

In its desire to create a balanced psychology of sexual relations, the ENR seeks to overcome the liabilities of conventional conservative thought: the perception of conservatives as joyless prudes, and the seemingly ridiculous psychology implied in conventional Christianity. It seeks to address "flesh-and-blood men and women," not saints. Since some of the Left's greatest gains in the last few decades have been made as a result of their championing sexual freedom and liberation, the ENR seeks to offer its own counter-ethic of sexual joy. The hope is presumably to nourish persons of the type who can, in Nietzsche's phrase, "make love after reading Hegel." This is also related to the desire for the reconciliation of the intellectual and warrior in one person: the reconciliation of vita contemplative and *vita activa*.[1]

It is therefore the task of contemporary proponents of the values of conservative revolution to create a body of sexual ethics that offers a genuine third position beyond that of mindless liberal

---

1    Wegierski, Mark. *The New Right in Europe.* Telos, Winter93/Spring94, Issue 98-99.

hedonism or the equally mindless sex-phobia of the Christian puritans. In working to cultivate such an alternative sexual ethos, the thought of Julius Evola regarding sexuality will be quite informative.

## The Evolan Worldview

Julius Evola published his *Eros and the Mysteries of Love: The Metaphysics of Sex* in 1958.[2] This work contains a comprehensive discussion of Evola's views of sexuality and the role of sexuality in his wider philosophical outlook. In the book, Evola provides a much greater overview of his own philosophy of sex, a philosophy which he had only alluded to in prior works such as *The Yoga of Power* (1949)[3] and, of course, his magnum opus *Revolt Against the Modern World* (1934)[4]. Evola's view of sexuality was very much in keeping with his wider view of history and civilization. Evola's philosophy, which he termed merely as "Tradition," was essentially a religion of Evola's own making. Evola's Tradition was a syncretic amalgam of various occult and metaphysical influences derived from ancient myths and esoteric writings. Foremost among these were the collection of myths found in various Greek and Hindu traditions having to do with a view of human civilization and culture as manifestation of a process of decline from a primordial "Golden Age."

It is interesting to note that Evola rejected modern views of evolutionary biology such as Darwinian natural selection. Indeed, his views on the origins of mankind overlapped with those of Vedic creationists within the Hindu tradition. This particular reflection of the Vedic tradition postulates the

---

2   Evola, Julius. *Eros and the Mysteries of Love: The Metaphysics of Sex*. English translation. New York: Inner Traditions, 1983. Originally published in Italy by Edizioni Mediterranee, 1969.

3   Evola, Julius. *The Yoga of Power: Tantra, Shakti, and the Secret Way*. English translation by Guido Stucci. New York: Inner Traditions, 1992. Originally published in 1949.

4   Evola, Julius. *Revolt Against the Modern World: Politics, Religion, and Social Order in the Kali Yuga*. English translation by Guido Stucco. New York: Inner Traditions, 1995. From the 1969 edition. Originally published in Milan by Hoepli in 1934.

concept of "devolution" which, at the risk of oversimplification, might be characterized as a spiritualistic inversion of modern notions of evolution. Mankind is regarded as having devolved into its present physical form from primordial spiritual beings, a view that is still maintained by some Hindu creationists in the contemporary world.[5] Comparable beliefs were widespread in ancient mythology. Hindu tradition postulates four "yugas" with each successive yuga marking a period of degeneration from the era of the previous yuga. The last of these, the so-called "Kali Yuga," represents an Age of Darkness that Evola appropriated as a metaphor for the modern world. This element of Hindu tradition parallels the mythical Golden Age of the Greeks, where the goddess of justice, Astraea, the daughter of Zeus and Themis, lived among mankind in an idyllic era of human virtue. The similarities of these myths to the legend of the Garden of Eden in the Abrahamic traditions where human beings lived in paradise prior the Fall are also obvious enough.

It would be easy enough for the twenty-first century mind to dismiss Evola's thought in this regard as a mere pretentious appeal to irrationality, mysticism, superstition or obscurantism. Yet to do so would be to ignore the way in which Evola's worldview represents a near-perfect spiritual metaphor for the essence of the thought of the man who was arguably the most radical and far-sighted thinker of modernity: Friedrich Nietzsche. Indeed, it is not implausible to interpret Evola's work as an effort to place the Nietzschean worldview within a wider cultural-historical and metaphysical framework that seeks to provide a kind of reconciliation with the essential features of the world's great religious traditions which have their roots in the early beginnings of human consciousness. Nietzsche, himself a radical materialist, likewise regarded the history of Western civilization as involving a process of degeneration from the high point of the pre-Socratic era. Both Nietzsche and Evola regarded modernity as the lowest yet achieved form of degenerative decadence with regards to

5    Cremo, Michael A. *Human Devolution: A Vedic Alternative to Darwin's Theory.* Torchlight Publishing, 2003.

expressions of human culture and civilization. The Nietzschean hope for the emergence of an *ubermenschen* that has overcome the crisis of nihilism inspired by modern civilization and the Evolan hope for a revival of primordial Tradition as an antidote to the perceived darkness of the current age each represent quite similar impulses within human thought.

## The Metaphysics of Sex

In keeping with his contemptuous view of modernity, Evola regarded modern sexual mores and forms of expression as degenerate. Just as Evola rejected modern evolutionary biology, so did he also oppose twentieth century approaches to the understanding of sexuality of the kind found in such fields as sociobiology, psychology, and the newly emergent discipline of sexology. Interestingly, Evola did not view the reproductive instinct in mankind to be the principal force driving sexuality and he criticized these academic disciplines for their efforts to interpret sexuality in terms of reproductive drives, regarding these efforts as a reflection of the materialistic reductionism which he so bitterly opposed. Evola's use of the term "metaphysics" with regards to sexuality represents in part his efforts to differentiate what he considered to be the "first principles" of human sexuality from the merely biological instinct for the reproduction of the species, which he regarded as being among the basest and least meaningful aspects of sex. It is also interesting to note at this point that Evola himself never married or had children of his own. Nor is it known to what degree his own paralysis generated by injuries sustained during World War Two as a result of a 1945 Soviet bombing raid on Vienna affected his own reproductive capabilities or his views of sexuality.

Perhaps the most significant aspect of Evola's analysis of sex is his rejection of not only the reproductive instinct but also of love as the most profound dimension of sexuality. Evola's thought on this matter is sharp departure from the dominant forces in traditional Western thought with regards to sexual ethics. Plato postulated a kind of love that transcends the sexual and rises above it, thereby remaining non-sexual in nature. The Christian tradition subjects the sexual impulse and act to a form of sacralization by which the process of creating life becomes a manifestation of the divine order. Hence, the traditional Christian taboos against non-procreative sexual acts. Modern humanism of a secular-liberal nature elevates romantic love to the highest form of sexual expression. Hence, the otherwise inexplicable phenomena of the modern liberal embrace of non-procreative, non-marital or even homosexual forms of sexual expression, while maintaining something of a taboo against forms of non-romantic sexual expression such as prostitution or forms of sexuality and sexual expression regarded as incompatible with the egalitarian ethos of liberalism, such as polygamy or "sexist" pornography.

Evola's own thought regarding sexuality diverges sharply from that of the Platonic ideal, the Christians, and the moderns alike. For Evola, sexuality has as its first purpose the achievement of unity in two distinctive ways. The first of these is the unity of the male and female dichotomy that defines the sexual division of the human species. Drawing once again on primordial traditions, Evola turns to the classical Greek myth of Hermaphroditus, the son of Hermes and Aphrodite who was believed to be a manifestation of both genders and who was depicted in the art of antiquity as having a male penis with female breasts in the same manner as the modern "she-male." The writings of Ovid depict Hermaphroditus as a beautiful young boy who was seduced by the nymph Salmacis and subsequently transformed into a male/female hybrid as a result of the union. The depiction of this story in the work of Theophrastus indicates that Hermaphroditus symbolized the marital union of a man and woman.

The concept of unity figures prominently in the Evolan view of sexuality on another level. Just as the sexual act is an attempt at reunification of the male and female division of the species, so is sexuality also an attempt to reunite the physical element of the human being with the spiritual. Again, Evola departs from the

Platonic, Christian, and modern views of sexuality. The classical and the modern overemphasize such characteristics as romantic love or aesthetic beauty in Evola's view, while the Christian sacralization of sexuality relegates the physical aspect to the level of the profane. However, Evola does not reject the notion of a profane dimension to sexuality. Instead, Evola distinguishes the profane from the transcendent. Profane expressions of sexuality are those of a non-transcendent nature. These can include both the hedonic pursuit of sexual pleasure as an end unto itself, but it also includes sexual acts with romantic love as their end.

Indeed, Evola's analysis of sexuality would be shockingly offensive to the sensibilities of traditionalists within the Abrahamic cults and those of modern liberal humanists alike. Evola is as forthright as any of the modern left-wing sexologists of his mid-twentieth century era (for instance, Alfred Kinsey[6] or Wilhelm Reich[7]) in the frankness of his discussion of the many dimensions of human sexuality, including sexual conduct of the most fringe nature. Some on the contemporary "far Right" of nationalist politics have attempted to portray Evola's view of homosexuality as the equivalent of that of a conventional Christian "homophobe." Yet a full viewing of Evola's writing on the homosexual questions does not lend itself to such an interpretation. The following passage from *The Metaphysics of Sex* is instructive on this issue:

> In natural homosexuality or in the predisposition to it, the most straightforward explanation is provided by what we said earlier about the differing levels of sexual development and about the fact that the process of sexual development in its physical and, even more so, in its psychic aspects can be incomplete. In that way, the original bisexual nature is surpassed to a lesser extent than in a "normal" human being, the characteristics of one sex not being predominant over those of the other sex to the same extent. Next we must

---

6    Pomeroy, Wardell. *Dr. Kinsey and the Institute for Sex Research.* New York: Harper & Row, 1972.

7    Sharaf, Myron. *Fury on Earth: A Biography of Wilhelm Reich.* Da Capo Press, 1994.

deal with what M. Hirschfeld called the "intermediate sexual forms." In cases of this kind (for instance, when a person who is nominally a man is only 60 percent male) it is impossible that the erotic attraction based on the polarity of the sexes in heterosexuality - which is much stronger the more the man is male and the woman is female - can also be born between individuals who, according to the birth registry and as regards only the so-called primary sexual characteristics, belong to the same sex, because in actual fact they are "intermediate forms". In the case of pederasts, Ulrich said rightly that it is possible to find "the soul of a woman born in the body of a man".

But it is necessary to take into account the possibility of constitutional mutations, a possibility that has been given little consideration by sexologists; that is, we must also bear in mind cases of regression. It may be that the governing power on which the sexual nature of a given individual depends (a nature that is truly male or truly female) may grow weak through neutralization, atrophy, or reduction of the latent state of the characteristics of the other sex, and this may lead to the activation and emergence of these recessive characteristics. And here the surroundings and the general atmosphere of society can play a not unimportant part. In a civilization where equality is the standard, where differences are not linked, where promiscuity is a favor, where the ancient idea of "being true to oneself" means nothing anymore - in such a splintered and materialistic society, it is clear that this phenomenon of regression and homosexuality should be particularly welcome, and therefore it is in no way a surprise to see the alarming increase in homosexuality and the "third sex" in the latest "democratic" period, or an increase in sex changes to an extent unparalleled in other eras.[8]

---

8    Evola, *Eros and the Mysteries of Love: The Metaphysics of Sex*, pp. 62-63.

In his recognition of the possibility of "the soul of a woman born in the body of man" or "intermediate" sexual forms, Evola's language and analysis somewhat resembles the contemporary cultural Left's fascination with the "transgendered" or the "intersexed." Where Evola's thought is to be most sharply differentiated from that of modern leftists is not on the matter of sex-phobia, but on the question of sexual egalitarianism. Unlike the Christian puritans who regard deviants from the heterosexual, procreative sexual paradigm as criminals against the natural order, Evola apparently understood the existence of such "sexual identities" as a naturally occurring phenomenon. Unlike modern liberals, Evola opposed the elevation of such sexual identities or practices to the level of equivalence with "normal" procreative and kinship related forms of sexual expression and relationship. On the contemporary question of same-sex marriage, for example, Evolan thought recognizes that the purpose of marriage is not individual gratification, but the construction of an institution for the reproduction of the species and the proliferation and rearing of offspring. An implication of Evola's thought on these questions for conservative revolutionaries in the twenty-first century is that the populations conventionally labeled as sexual deviants by societies where the Abrahamic cults shape the wider cultural paradigm need not be shunned, despised, feared, or subject to persecution. Homosexuals, for instance, have clearly made important contributions to Western civilization. However, the liberal project of elevating either romantic love or hedonic gratification as the highest end of sexuality, and of equalizing "normal" and "deviant" forms of sexual expression, must likewise be rejected if relationships between family, tribe, community, and nation are to be understood as the essence of civilization.

The nature of Evola's opposition to modern pornography and the relationship of this opposition to his wider thought regarding sexuality is perhaps the most instructive with regards to the differentiation to be made between Evola's outlook and that of Christian moralists. Evola's opposition to pornography was not its explicit nature or its deviation from procreative, marital expressions of sexuality as the idealized norm. Indeed, Evola highly regarded sexual practices of a ritualized nature, including orgiastic religious rites of the kind found in certain forms of paganism, to be among the most idyllic forms of sexual expression of the highest, spiritualized variety. Christian puritans of the present era might well find Evola's views on these matters to be even more appalling than those of ordinary contemporary liberals. Evola also considered ritualistic or ascetic celibacy to be such an idyllic form. The basis of Evola's objection to pornography was its baseness, its commercial nature, and its hedonic ends, all of which Evola regarding as diminishing its erotic nature to the lowest possible level. Evola would no doubt regard the commercialized hyper-sexuality that dominates the mass media and popular culture of the Western world of the twenty-first century as a symptom rather than as a cause of the decadence of modernity.

# Aleister Crowley

## The Whole of the Law:
## The Political Dimensions of Crowley's Thought

The fame of Aleister Crowley is principally derived from his reputation as a notorious occultist. It is this reputation that has made his name legendary in numerous counter-cultural and youth culture circles, ranging from contemporary enthusiasts for witchcraft of varying sorts to purveyors of certain shades of heavy metal music. Yet for all his status as a legendary figure, Crowley is not typically regarded as a political thinker. To the degree that his ideas are considered relevant to political thought at all, Crowley is frequently caricatured as a shallow nihilist or merely as a debauched libertine. Extremist political subcultures of varying stripes have attempted to claim him as one of their own. Whether they are neo-fascists, egocentric individualists, or nihilist pseudo-anarchists, many with an extremist political outlook have attempted to shock the broader bourgeois society by invoking the name of Aleister Crowley. This state of affairs regarding Crowley's political outlook is unfortunate, because an examination of the man's political ideas reveals him to be a far more profound and insightful thinker on such questions than what is typically recognized.

It is indeed understandable that divergent political factions would attempt to claim Crowley for themselves, given that his political thought is rather difficult to classify and cannot be reconciled with any established ideological paradigm. His ideas and pronouncements on political matters have to be understood within the wider context of his thought and worldview. Merely citing a quotation or opinion on some matter issued by Crowley here or there is to invite the risk of misrepresenting the wider body of his thought by assuming his association with some particular ideology or philosophical stance with which he did not identify. Crowley's ideas have been particularly misrepresented in the United States, a nation that differs from most other industrialized countries and virtually all other nations of the Western world in that it possesses a large population of religious fundamentalists. The large Protestant evangelical subculture in the United States includes within itself a substantial number of people who continue to believe in the reality of the powers of witchcraft and in the existence of Satan as a literal personal being who acts as an evil supernatural force within the natural world. This subculture contains within itself an abundance of sensational literature and small-time demagogues claiming to have identified some form of evil occult force operating in the broader society through secretive organizations or through the manipulation of forms of popular culture such as film, the arts, television, rock n' roll music, pornography, and the like.[1] Within the literature and rhetoric of this subculture, the name of Aleister Crowley is often used almost as a synonym for evil and Satanic forces.

The obscurantism and ignorance demonstrated by these elements often produces an ironic result. Parallel to the religious subculture of those warning of imminent dangers posed by occult forces of the kind supposedly represented by the likes of Crowley is a corresponding youth culture built up around an occult mystique utilizing many of the same names and symbols that figure prominently in the shrill hysteria of the Christian fundamentalists. The reigning principle of social psychology operating here is one where the occult mystique is presented by the demagogues and sensationalists in the standard manner of the "forbidden fruit," which defiantly rebellious, independently minded, or merely curious youth subsequently seek to consume. Hence, the proliferation of such youth culture phenomena

---

1    Victor, Jeffrey S. *Satanic Panic: The Creation of a Contemporary Legend*. Open Court Publishing Company, 1993.

as heavy metal rock bands with demonic names and song lyrics, and displaying occult symbols as a logo. That Crowley never identified himself as a Satanist and that his religion of Thelema is hardly a variation of Satanic thought (even if some self-styled contemporary Thelemites also fancy themselves as Satanists) is a fact that is often completely lost to these cultural undercurrents.[2] Just as Crowley's religious thought has been so badly misunderstood or misinterpreted, Crowley's thought on political matters has suffered similar abuses.

# Do What Thou Wilt

Perhaps no aspect of Crowley's thinking has been more misunderstood than his famous pronouncement: *"Do what thou wilt shall be the whole of the law."*[3] Widely cited by critics and supposed admirers of Crowley alike as an incitement to anti-social egocentrism or as mere nihilism manifesting itself as a kind of adolescent-like rebellion, this passage is given such amateurish interpretations by those who completely ignore or misunderstand the concept of "the will" in Crowley's outlook. For Crowley, the notion of "the will" is something of a synonym for the destiny of the individual which is built into the metaphysical fabric of the cosmos. Yet, Crowley was not a fatalist, and "the will" should not be confused with "fate" in the sense of some inevitable outcome pre-ordained by a providential or supernatural force. The will is something an individual must discover for himself through introspective, spiritual, or esoteric pursuits. The Crowleyan concept of "the will" is remarkably similar to the Nietzschean idea of "the will to power" in that it involves a form of self-overcoming and ascension to a form of existence that is greater than concern with mundane human pursuits or enslavement to base desires. This aspect of Crowley's spirituality might also be compared to the meditative pursuits found in the Eastern traditions. To find one's "true will" is to

---

2     Rabinovitch, Shelley; Lewis, James. *The Encyclopedia of Modern Witchcraft and Neo-Paganism.* Citadel Press, 2004, pp. 267-270

3     Crowley, Liber Legis (*"The Book of the Law"*). Maine: Samuel Weiser, 1976, 2: 25.

find one's "calling." An elitist, Crowley regarded the discovery of one's "true will" as something only the special few were capable of achieving. Such people are those who shine brighter than the rest of humanity. Crowley used the analogy of a star to describe the individual human personality. For Crowley, all people are stars, but some stars shine much greater than others.[4]

One of Crowley's most important works was *The Book of the Law*, which appeared in 1904. Crowley claimed that this work had been dictated to him orally during a stay in Egypt by a spiritual being called Aiwass, who became Crowley's Holy Guardian Angel and who was the messenger of the ancient Greek god Horus and two other deities. *The Book of the Law* is supposedly the record of that dictation.[5] The mind of a contemporary Western intellectual would no doubt be inclined to immediately dismiss such a claim as mere quackery or charlatanry. However, it must be recognized that the claims of Crowley regarding his having received supposed revelation from Horus differ in no significant way from those of similar claims found in many of the world's great religious traditions or in forms of popular or contemporary religion possessing substantial numbers of adherents. The Islamic tradition maintains similar claims regarding the revelation of the *Koran* to the Prophet Muhammed. The evangelical Protestant tradition in which Crowley himself was raised likewise regards the *Bible* as having been revealed to its authors by means of divine inspiration. Crowley's claim of having received special knowledge contained in *The Book of the Law* resembles as well Joseph Smith's claim of having discovered the sacred text of the *Book of Mormon*. Lastly, Crowley's supposed encounter with the being of Aiwass greatly resembles the practice of "trance channeling" common to some contemporary "New Age" religious practices. In other words, the spiritual claims of Crowley and his followers should not necessarily be dismissed as any less credible or fantastic than comparable spiritual beliefs held by persons and

---

4    Bolton, Kerry. *Aleister Crowley as Political Theorist, Part I*. Counter-Currents. Counter-Currents Publishing, September 2, 2010.

5    Crowley, Aleister. *The Equinox of the Gods*. New Falcon Publications, 1991.

religious communities possessing greater numbers of adherents or higher levels of political or cultural respectability. Crowley's religion of Thelema is properly regarded as a contemporary pagan, polytheistic counterpart to these rival religious systems.

# The Political and Social Context of Crowley's Thought

Aleister Crowley originated from the British upper-middle class. His father's family owned a successful brewing business thereby making Aleister, born in 1875 and originally named Edward Alexander Crowley, a child of the classical British bourgeoisie of the late nineteenth century. His parents were converts to a fundamentalist brand of evangelical Protestantism, a faith which Aleister became skeptical of and rejected while still in his teens. His father died when he was only eleven, and while Crowley later referred to his late father as his friend and hero, it is known that his relationship with his mother became rather strained, though the source of the family conflict is not specifically known. As a university student, Crowley became a sexual adventurer, pursuing sexual relationships with prostitutes and other promiscuous young women he met in seedy locations, and began experimenting with homosexuality as well. That Crowley would devote his adult life to the pursuit of activities regarded as extreme taboos by the sectarian religious environment of his upbringing motivates one to consider the question of to what degree his early family and religious experiences influenced his later outlook. A Freudian might be inclined to regard Crowley's fascination with sex, drugs, and the occult as stemming from a compulsion to differentiate his own identity from the sacred beliefs of a mother he apparently greatly disliked. Likewise, the ability of sectarian religious communities to provoke rebellion on the part of those initially indoctrinated into their tenants during their formative years is well-documented. One can only speculate as to the nature of the impact of such experiences on Crowley.[6]

---

6    Sutin, Laurence. *Do What Thou Wilt: A Life of Aleister Crowley.* Macmillan, 2000;
     Kaczynksi, Richard. Perdurabo: *The Life of Aleister Crowley* (Second Edition). Berkeley,

Crowley's thought on political and social matters resembles greatly that of a number of thinkers who emerged in the first half of the twentieth century as critics of the modern industrial era and its cultural impact. The industrial civilization of modernity had brought with it an exponential population growth, a greatly expanded middle class, an increasingly commercialized society, and a dramatic increase in urbanization. Political ideologies like liberalism, democracy, and socialism became increasingly influential and began to shape the nature of modern statecraft. The principal cultural impact of these developments was the uprooting or dislocation of many aspects of traditional society and the growth of a new kind of mass society comprised of workers, consumers, professionals, technicians, businessmen, journalists, and politicians. These dramatic changes were alarming to their critics for a variety of reasons. Conservatives of different types saw such social developments as undermining traditional forms of authority and social cohesion, and thereby generating anomie, crime, hedonism, impiety and the like due to the decline of the fixed social norms associated with more traditional social institutions.

These criticisms were, of course, not unlike those of contemporary social conservatives. However, another criticism of modernity advanced by such thinkers is one that is now less well known and would likely be considered quaint, archaic, or even viciously retrograde by the modern liberal mind. Some were also concerned with the impact of the growth of mass society, commercialization, urbanization, and egalitarian political values on high culture and on the natural elites. Of course, one of the earliest and most profound critics of modernity of this kind was Nietzsche. Subsequent thinkers of this type included a number of individuals whose own thought was often markedly different from one another. Such intellectuals included Auberon Herbert, H.L. Mencken, Hilaire Belloc, Jose Ortega y Gasset, Vifredo Pareto, Julius Evola, Ernst Junger, Rene Guenon,

California: North Atlantic Books, 2010.

J.R.R. Tolkien, Erik von Kuehnelt-Leddihn, Aldous Huxley, and Bertrand De Jouvenal. Also representative of this kind of thinking were a number of French writers and intellectuals associated with a tendency that has been called "anarchisme de droite," or "anarchism of the right." Among these were Édouard Drumont, Barbey d'Aurevilly, Paul Léautaud, Louis Pauwels, and Louis-Ferdinand Céline.[7]

Different though their specific outlooks may have been, a common thread in the thinking of these critics of modernity was their rejection of the belief in innate human equality inherent in the rising ideological forces of the era. The advent of mass democracy, universal suffrage, and parliamentary politics was regarded by these thinkers as the replacement of statesmanship with mob rule. The trend towards universal education was seen not as a means of uplifting the ignorant masses but as a process of lowering those of superior ability and intelligence to the level of the mediocre. The commercialization of culture and society and the corresponding growth of the mass media were seen as diminishing the significance and prominence of traditional forms of high culture in favor of the lowbrow manifestations of popular culture that now dominate contemporary societies. Yet another concern advanced by this strand of thought was related to the effect of mass democracy, mass society, and egalitarian values on individual liberty.

Contemporary liberals habitually assume that liberty and democracy are synonymous with one another, or at least share a complementary role. More cogent or perceptive thinkers have understood the inherent tension between egalitarianism and liberty. The modern democratic state, for instance, ultimately places the fate of the individual's well-being in the hands of the shifting whims of popular opinion and equally shifting coalitions of fickle and narrowly-focused special interest groups. Efforts to eradicate inequality have led to the phenomenal growth of

7    Ollivier-Mellio, Anne. H.L. Mencken: Anarchist of the Right? *Attack the System*, November 24, 2009.

the state and the ever escalating intrusion of the state into areas of society where political interference was previously regarded as taboo. These earlier proponents of aristocratic individualism were often quite prophetic in their diagnosis of the predictable political consequences of radically egalitarian ideologies. It is to this strand of now somewhat obscure thought regarding political and social questions that Aleister Crowley himself belongs.

## Crowley's Aristocratic Radicalism

Though of bourgeoisie origins, Crowley regarded the commercial values of capitalism to be incompatible with genuine elitism. Like others who shared a similar critique of modernity, Crowley regarded the elevation of the business class to the status of the ruling class as a form of social degeneration. Like Nietzsche and Junger, he championed the decline of bourgeoisie society and hoped for its replacement with a new kind of nobility. Crowley obviously differed from Christian traditionalists who objected to modernity mostly because of its success at undermining the authority of the Church. Indeed, Crowley predictably admired previous anticlerical tendencies such as Freemasonry and even declared the Illuminati founder Adam Weishaupt to be one of the saints of Thelema. Yet Crowley's outlook was hardly compatible with the egalitarian ideals of modernity that grew out of the French Revolution. No less than Julius Evola, for instance, recognized many of Crowley's ideas as compatible with his own religion of Tradition.[8] Some of Crowley's views resembled those of the Social Darwinists.

Few statements of Crowley summarize the nature of his aristocratic radicalism with more clarity that these:

> "It is the evolutionary and natural view . . . Nature's way is to weed out the weak. This is the most merciful way too. At present all the strong are being damaged, and their progress being hindered by the dead weight of the weak

---

8    Bolton, Kerry. *Aleister Crowley as Political Theorist, Part I*. Counter-Currents. Counter-Currents Publishing, September 2, 2010.

limbs and the missing limbs, the diseased limbs and the atrophied limbs. The Christians to the lions."[9]

"And when the trouble begins, we aristocrats of freedom, from the castle to the cottage, the tower or the tenement, shall have the slave mob against us."[10]

"We are not for the poor and sad: the lords of the earth are our kinsfolk. Beauty and strength, leaping laughter, and delicious languor, force and fire are of us . . . we have nothing to do with the outcast and unfit. For they feel not. Compassion is the vice of kings; stamp down the wretched and the weak: this is the law of the strong; this is our law and the joy of the world."[11]

Yet for all of his championing of the superior man over the mediocrities, the strong over the weak, and the special few against the inconsequential many, Crowley was not a proponent of tyranny or injustice. He opposed the totalitarian ideologies of Communism, Fascism, and National Socialism which arose during his lifetime.[12] Like many anti-modernist or anti-egalitarian thinkers of the time, including even the classical liberal Ludwig von Mises[13] and the anarchist Peter Kropotkin[14], Crowley engaged in a brief flirtatious fascination with Mussolini

---

9     Crowley, Aleister. *The Law Is For All*. Arizona: Falcon Press, 1985, p. 175.

10    *Ibid.*, p. 192.

11    Liber Legis 2: 17–21.

12    *Aleister Crowley on Politics*. The Arcane Archives. http://www.arcane-archive.org/religion/thelema/aleister-crowley-on-politics-1.php Accessed on April 5, 2011.

13    Mises, Ludwig von. Liberalism. 1927. Said Mises: "It cannot be denied that Fascism and similar movements aiming at the establishment of dictatorships are full of the best intentions and that their intervention has, for the moment, saved European civilization. The merit that Fascism has thereby won for itself will live on eternally in history. But though its policy has brought salvation for the moment, it is not of the kind which could promise continued success. Fascism was an emergency makeshift. To view it as something more would be a fatal error."

14    Anduril, Victor. Anarchic Philosophy. *Attack the System*. http://attackthesystem.com/anarchic-philosophy-by-victor-anduril/Accessed on April 5, 2011.Said Kropotkin of Mussolini: "I am delighted by his boldness."

when the *fascisti* first emerged as a political force, but soon came to reconsider such sympathies. Indeed, Crowley had established a Thelemite commune in Sicily in 1920 which was subsequently closed by the Mussolini government three years later with Crowley himself being expelled from Italy.[15]

Like many intellectuals who were concerned with the effects of modernity and a commercialized society on high culture, Crowley understood that the growth of human culture had historically been intertwined with the growth of a leisure class. In traditional societies, it had been the aristocracy that comprised the leisure class and therefore devoted much of its energy to cultural pursuits. Like comparable thinkers of the era, Crowley understood that the decline of traditional aristocracies in favor of a society comprised of businessmen and laborers devoted to the pursuit of mere profit or sustenance conflicted with the maintenance of a culture-producing leisure class. Therefore, Crowley became attracted to systems of economic thought that offered a third way beyond egalitarian socialism and the commercial values of capitalism. A number of ideologies of this kind emerged during Crowley's era from both the Left and the Right. These included Guild Socialism, Syndicalism, Catholic Distributism, Social Credit, and the worker-soldier state promoted by Ernst Junger and the National-Bolshevik Ernst Niekisch. Crowley himself outlined a similar scheme for his ideal Thelemic state. Like the proponents of Guild Socialism and Syndicalism, Crowley favored a parliamentary system with representation based on profession and occupation rather than geography.[16] Crowley described his proposed system in these terms:

> Before the face of the Areopagus stands an independent Parliament of the Guilds. Within the Order, irrespective of Grade, the members of each craft, trade, science, or

15   Bolton, Kerry. *Aleister Crowley as Political Theorist, Part II*. Counter-Currents. Counter-Currents Publishing, September 3, 2010.

16   Ibid.

profession form themselves into a Guild, making their own laws, and prosecute their own good, in all matters pertaining to their labor and means of livelihood. Each Guild chooses the man most eminent in it to represent it before the Areopagus of the Eighth Degree; and all disputes between the various Guild are argued before that Body, which will decide according to the grand principles of the Order. Its decisions pass for ratification to the Sanctuary of the Gnosis, and thence to the Throne.[17]

The esoteric terminology in the above statement aside, the pagan occultist Crowley was essentially advocating the same system of economic governance as the Catholic traditionalists G. K. Chesterton and Hilaire Belloc.

Regarding the structure of the state itself, like most proponents of aristocratic individualism, Crowley was a monarchist. He believed that the duties of government itself should be conducted by a non-elected Senate. The Senate would be chosen by an Electoral College appointed by the King. Crowley's idea of the Electoral College was a conceptually interesting institution that was essentially a kind of political monastery. Members of the Electoral College would commit themselves to a vow of poverty, and be selected from the ranks of volunteers who had previously exhibited excellence in fields of scholarship, the arts, or athletics.[18] One might guess that a man such as Crowley who engaged in so many pursuits that were in defiance of the social or even legal norms of his time would not favor a form of political government prone to arbitrary or intrusive interference in individual lives. Regarding matters of law, Crowley was for the most part a libertarian. He succinctly described this outlook in the *Book of the Law*:

---

17   Crowley, Aleister. Liber CXCIV, "O.T.O. An Intimation with Reference to the Constitution of the Order," paragraph 21, *The Equinox*, vol. III, no. 1, 1919.

18   Bolton, Kerry. *Aleister Crowley as Political Theorist, Part II*. Counter-Currents. Counter-Currents Publishing, September 3, 2010.

Man has the right to live by his own law— to live in the way that he wills to do: to work as he will: to play as he will: to rest as he will: to die when and how he will. Man has the right to eat what he will: to drink what he will: to dwell where he will: to move as he will on the face of the earth. Man has the right to think what he will: to speak what he will: to write what he will: to draw, paint, carve, etch, mould, build as he will: to dress as he will. Man has the right to love as he will:… "take your fill and will of love as ye will, when, where, and with whom ye will." Man has the right to kill those who would thwart these rights.[19]

While Crowley was clearly not an anarchist or a libertarian in the sense of a modern bourgeois liberal, the above statement is in its essence as much a libertarian-anarchistic creed as any ever issued. For Crowley, the chief aim of politics was to afford every individual the opportunity for the discovery and realization of their "True Will" tempered with cautious recognition that only the superior few will succeed in such pursuits. One might be tempted to compare the ideal Thelemic state of Aleister Crowley with Max Stirner's idealized "Union of Egoists" or, obviously, Nietzsche's hope for the ascension of an *ubermensch*.

The political thought of Aleister Crowley retains its relevance to the present era in the same manner that the thought of his contemporaries who shared similar or overlapping views and critiques of modernity remains relevant. The ongoing process of decay of Western cultural and political institutions becomes increasingly evident with each subsequent generation. The currently reigning ideology in Western society is a synthesis of mass democracy, economism, and an increasingly nihilistic and absurdist form of radical egalitarianism. The political tyranny and cultural destructiveness inherent in such an ideological framework will continue to become ever more obvious to greater numbers of people. Two great questions will emerge from this

---

19   Crowley, Aleister. Duty. http://lib.oto-usa.org/crowley/essays/duty.html. Accessed on April 5, 2011.

crisis: "What went wrong?" and "What might an alternative be?" Aleister Crowley is yet another thinker from the past who saw the crisis in advance and who might be considered as yet another possible source of inspiration and guidance in the future.

# *Corneliu Codreanu*

## Corneliu Codreanu and the Warrior Ethos

European civilization of the early to middle twentieth century was characterized in part by the growth of political movements with a martial character. These included both the many variants of fascism from the far Right and revolutionary socialist currents from the far Left. The proliferation of such movements accelerated sharply in the interwar period. Particularly noteworthy were Mussolini's *Fascisti* and the National Socialists of Germany, given the later success of these at actual achievement of state power, as well as the various factions involved in the Spanish Civil War. Romania's Iron Guard, under the leadership of Corneliu Codreanu, was unique among these movements in that it was one of the few such tendencies with a strong religious orientation, and a highly eccentric religiosity at that. (Payne, 1995)

The religiosity of the Iron Guard is ironic given that the rise of secular mass movements with a strong martial or even apocalyptic outlook during the twentieth century can easily be interpreted as a substitution for declining religious enthusiasms during the same era. Nietzsche had predicted that the twentieth-century would be a time of great ideological wars, and history has demonstrated the prescience of Nietzsche's prediction. Yet, Nietzsche regarded the ominous cloud of previously unparalleled warfare he saw on the horizon as a consequential phase through which humanity must pass in part due to the "death of God" and the quest for new gods to fill the resulting void. While Nietzsche himself detested militarism, he also lamented the decline of the warrior ethos in the era of modernity. Like Ernst Junger after him, Nietzsche considered the comforts of bourgeois society to have brought with them an emasculating aversion to danger and a pervasive preoccupation with safety and security. These observations were the foundation of the underlying sentiments expressed in the Nietzschean adage that "a good fight justifies any cause." (Preston, 2011; Junger,)

The twentieth century certainly brought with it a myriad of causes which inspired their adherents to "a good fight." While the icons of Race, Nation, or Class largely replaced "God" in the pantheons of twentieth century secularized religiosity, it was among the ranks of Codreanu's Iron Guard (or the Legion of the Archangel Michael, as the Guard also referred to itself) that the older icons of God, Faith, and Church retained their traditional place. Indeed, it was perhaps among the Iron Guard that martial values achieved extremes that were unparalleled among other ideological revolutionaries of the era. Of all the extremist movements of the period, the Iron Guard surpassed perhaps even the German *S.A.* in the development of a cult of death and martyrdom. The similarities between German National Socialism and the Iron Guard were great. The particularly obvious parallels are the virulent nationalism, anti-communism, and anti-Semitism of both movements. Codreanu could fairly be said to have rivaled Hitler in the fervor of his anti-Jewish rhetoric. (Volovici, 1991)

However, perhaps the most interesting dimension of the ideology of the Iron Guard was its approach to theology. The Legionnaires conceived of the Romanian nation as having a special relationship to God and its commitment to the traditional Orthodox Christianity of the Romanian people informed every aspect of their thought and action. Like Ignatius Loyola, the founder of the ruthlessly Catholic Jesuit order before them, the Legionnaires recognized no limitations on the ends to which they might go in defense of their particular variation of the Christian faith. The extremism of their cult of martyrdom is perhaps best exemplified by their belief that in order to defend the Faith and the Nation, a Legionnaire might at times be called upon to perform deeds that would result in his own damnation. In other words, not only an individual life but an individual soul must at times be sacrificed for the greater good of the struggle. This is likely the most intense form of cultic martyrdom ever devised. Religious movements which teach martyrdom typically promise reward in a future life for the faithful holy warrior who sacrifices his mere mortal life for the cause. Yet for the holy warriors of the Iron Guard, a soldier of faith could be called upon to lay down not only his mortal life but his immortal soul as well. (Payne, 1995) No cult of martyrdom could ever be more extreme. Their fervent Orthodoxy aside, one might be tempted to compare the theological outlook of the Legionnaires with that of Milton's Lucifer. Just as Milton depicted Satan as having insisted that it is better to rule in Hell than serve in Heaven, so might the faithful warriors of the Iron Guard be said to have believed that it is better to achieve Hell in the struggle for one's nation than to achieve Heaven for having engaged in a less virulent struggle. The Romanian warriors took the martyrdom cults of the Islamic jihadists or the Japanese kamikazes still a step further.

Because of their stalwart religiosity and fervent attachment to Romanian tradition, it is also tempting to dismiss the Legionnaires as mere reactionaries of the throne and altar variety rather than to recognize them as a manifestation of an authentic revolutionary force in European civilization of the time. Yet such a conclusion would be problematical. As early as 1919, Codreanu himself had joined Constantin Pancu's National Awareness Guard, a right-wing anti-communist faction that simultaneously advocated for greater worker rights. Likewise, the Iron Guard itself was involved in the organization of cooperatives and, like many radical right movements of the era, voiced fervent opposition to both capitalism and communism. (Barbu, 1993) In many ways the Iron Guard might be considered an Orthodox counterpart to the Falangist movement of Spain's Jose Antonio Primo de Rivera. The ideological parallels are rather significant. Both movements espoused a radical nationalist philosophy that attacked communism, finance capital, liberalism, internationalism, and parliamentarism and while expressing support for the traditional faith of the people of their respective nations. Both maintained a primary orientation towards paramilitarism and armed struggle in a way that represented the evolution of the Right beyond the throne and altar reactionary current towards a genuinely revolutionary nationalism. (Rivera, 1936) Yet both movements maintained an outlook that was more traditional than the modernist influences exhibited by some radical right movements of the era, such as the anticlericalism of the German National Socialists, the *avant-garde* influences on Italian Fascism, the Nietzscheanism of the Conservative Revolutionaries, or the Marxism of the National-Bolsheviks. In other ways, the Iron Guard resembled the now forgotten anti-communist Buddhist or Catholic militias formed in the nations of Indochina during the early period of the civil wars in those nations.

The prevalence of so many forces exhibiting an uncompromising martial spirit throughout the Western world in the first half of the twentieth century is all the more remarkable given the near total disappearance of martial values in Western culture of the present time. The militaries of the contemporary Western nations are barely militaries at all but instead function as glorified police departments forever being deployed in the pursuit of dubious and never-ending "peacekeeping" and "humanitarian" endeavors. Even the massive military-industrial complex maintained by the United States functions more as a corporate welfare scheme for legions of crony capitalists connected to the American state. American military personnel are careerist bureaucrats rivaling their counterparts in the civilian sectors of the state or the world of capitalist corporations. Indeed, even among the rank and file, the military forces of the United States are more a collection of mercenaries and fraternities than anything that could be said to exhibit a warrior ethos in the historic or traditional sense. The blending of modern warfare and high-technology has served in many ways to eliminate the truly martial aspects of warfare. Instead, the forces of the American empire and its allies drop bombs from the safety of the skies. "War" for these modern imperial legions is sometimes more comparable to a visit to a video arcade than engagement on the battlefield. Indeed, the American military now serves a primary force for the perpetration of Political Correctness as represented by its conscientious commitment to "diversity," properly integrating women and homosexuals into its ranks, and upholding "human rights" on a global scale rather than cultivating a warrior ethos or upholding its own historic traditions. (Hunter, 2009)

One is inclined to wonder what Western civilization might be today if its recent ancestors who did indeed exhibit such martial valor had not simultaneously squandered so much blood and treasure in internecine warfare over petty nationalisms, sectarian ideological squabbles, and class hatreds. Whether they were the Legionnaires of Romania, the Falangists of Spain, the Brownshirts of Germany, the Blackshirts of Italy, the Anarchists of Catalonia, or the Communist street fighters of the KPD, it seems a pity that so much blood was lost in struggles that were ultimately futile and meaningless and that these struggles eventually culminated in explosive and historically unrivaled warfare that ended the reign of Europe as the world's premiere civilization in favor of the American hegemony that has dominated since 1945. One wonders if such martial spirit could ever again be recaptured and directed towards a more constructive vision. The decadence of modern society is illustrated by the apathetic nature of its population. The principal values of contemporary Western culture are the pursuit of material comfort, safety, and personal hedonism. Only a dramatic psychic sea change among Western peoples generated by necessity would likely reverse this prevailing trend.

It appears that just as the torch of politico-economic dominance and cultural evolution is currently being passed from Europe to Asia, so is the torch of martial spirit and the warrior ethos being passed to the insurgent forces of the Third World. The spirit of the Legionnaires continues to thrive not among Western Christians but among Islamic insurgents originating from

Asia, Africa, and the Middle East and the remaining armed struggle movements of Latin America. Today's holy warriors are Islamists rather than Legionnaires or Falangists. It is the Muslim insurgents who now raise the banner of the classical Anarchist ideal of "propaganda by the deed." (Hari, 2009) It is the youth of the Muslim nations rather than Western youth who fight the institutions of decadent, corrupt and archaic authorities in the streets. Indeed, virtually the only elements demonstrating any sort of martial values in contemporary Western society are lumpenproletarian street gangs.

The most advanced military theorists of the contemporary era have recognized the dramatic changes that are currently evolving on a global basis concerning the nature of war. Commonly labeled as "fourth generation warfare," the new form which human martial endeavor assumes is that involving non-state actors. This is a genuinely revolutionary phenomenon that is essentially overturning the monopoly on the waging of war assigned to the state since the time of the Treaty of Westphalia. War is now waged not by states but by movements lacking state power or which have replaced state power in a situation of political collapse. Among the most prominent example of these is Lebanon's Hezbollah militia which essentially serves as the defense force of the otherwise militarily impotent Lebanese nation, having successful repelled the Israeli invasion in the summer of 2006. Hezbollah has likewise assumed the domestic as well as external roles normally played by conventional states with its provision of public health, education, and welfare services. (Preston, 2006) Ironically, it might well be said that Hezbollah is the closest parallel to the Iron Guard of any contemporary political or military movement.

It is clear enough the legacy of Corneliu Codreanu and the Iron Guard, like the legacy of so many comparable movements of the era, belongs to the past. However admirable the personal valor of Codreanu and his Legionnaires may have been, there can be no doubt that many of the ideas that fueled their movement have become increasingly archaic with the passing of time. For instance, their adherence to the model of the Jewish conspiracy outlined in the "Protocols of the Elders of Zion" now seems a bit primitive, and one need not be an adherent of the pieties of contemporary political correctness to recognize the anti-Jewish rhetoric and actions of the Legionnaires as inordinately extreme. Likewise, one may find the alleged mystical nature of the relationship between the Orthodox faith and the Romanian nation championed by the faithful of the Iron Guard to be dubious in nature. The era of such extreme fidelity to a particular nation-state has certainly passed and conventional patriotism of the kind assigned to historic nation-states becomes increasingly less prevalent in the contemporary world. Likewise, the decline of orthodox or traditional Christian religious belief of any kind among Westerners is well known. It is doubtful that either Christianity or national patriotism could ever again inspire the inhabitants of Western civilization in the way these inspired those of previous eras. Clearly, these things are relics from the past. Valuable relics they may be, perhaps, but relics nevertheless. (Van Creveld, 1999)

Yet as Western civilization continues its process of decline, it is likely that its indigenous peoples will once again be in search of identity as a result of the dislocation generated by the collapse of their civilization. As the current century unfolds and Asian preeminence becomes ever more obvious and the demographic overrun of the West becomes ever more imminent, it is likely that the primordial spirits of Western peoples will once again awaken. At that point, the indigenous peoples of the West will become insurgents once again and may well come to resemble present insurgents of the Third World. When such an era arrives, indigenous Europeans will no doubt look to find inspiration from past figures representing the martial spirit and warrior ethos that Westerners once took for granted. It is certainly possible that Corneliu Codreanu will be one among many such figures.

# *Alain De Benoist*

"Whoever invokes humanity wants to cheat."
–Pierre Joseph Proudhon

## The Essentials of the European New Right

It was my discovery of the European New Right that finally convinced me that one could be both a serious intellectual and a political rightist. My initiation came when I discovered Alain De Benoist's and Charles Champetier's manifesto for the French New Right in 2000. I had never seen rightist ideas presented in such a way before and I knew I had come upon something powerful. Previously, I had been more or less a left-wing Chomskyite. I had long found the left dissatisfying, particularly its victimological ressentiment and its Politically Correct bluenoses. Yet, when I looked at the bulk of the American right and saw the jingoist flag-wavers, Bible-bangers, Israel-firsters, plutocratic apologists, conspiracists, and knee-jerk militarists, I would wonder why would anyone could possibly want to be associated with that, for God's sake? Murray Rothbard's championing of the legacy of the "Old Right" notwithstanding, I considered the right to be an intellectual wasteland. Fortunately, the European New Right rescued me from such a narrow perception. It was from the European New Right that I learned one could be a progressive without being an egalitarian, a conservative without succumbing to vulgar economism, and a traditionalist without being a yahoo.

A major problem with bringing ENR ideas to North American audiences has been the fact that much of the scholarship produced by ENR writers has yet to be translated into English. For instance, De Benoist is the leading intellectual of the ENR and one of its founding fathers, yet only two of De Benoist's dozens of books, *On Being a Pagan* and *The Problem of Democracy*, have undergone an English translation and the latter appeared in English only this year thanks to Arktos Publishing. Two original English works surveying ENR thought have also appeared. One of these is by Tomislav Sunic and the other is by Michael O'Meara. If one is a college student and wants to shock and offend politically correct professors and peers, then the distribution of copies of these works on campuses would certainly be an easy way to do so.

Because of the efforts of Arktos, more and more works of the ENR are gradually being made available in English as well as older works originally written by long-forgotten conservative revolutionary figures of the interwar era. Arktos also makes available works by leftist thinkers offering genuine insight and other writers whose ideas fall way outside the paradigm of what passes for "the right" within the context of U.S. style "conservatism." Suffice to say we will not be seeing any of the plutocrat-funded and neocon-managed publishing houses of America's "conservative movement" issuing the works of Lothrop Stoddard, Antonio Gramsci, Georges Sorel, Carl Schmitt, Michael Cremo, Andrew Fraser, or Pentti Linkola. Arktos has also issued an English version of Ernst von Salomon's *It Cannot Be Stormed*. Salomon was a conservative revolutionary author whose success continued well into the post-WW2 period and earned the denunciation of TIME magazine in the process. I am still waiting for English translations of Ernst Junger's *Der Arbeiter* and of the works of Ernst Niekisch.

Several contemporary works by leading ENR writers, such as Alain De Benoist, Tomislav Sunic, and Guillame Faye have been given extensive reviews by English reviewers. Sunic's *Against Democracy and Equality* is particularly helpful not only as an introduction to ENR ideas on a more abstract level, but as a source of critical insights that shed extensive light on the realities behind some of the more important political and cultural phenomena of our time. As Brett Stevens observes in his review of Sunic:

Liberalism dehumanizes its adversaries. According to Carl Schmitt as channeled through Sunic, the left abhors war — so it phrases every political action as a police action. The bad guys become inhuman because they are immoral, not nice, not egalitarian, etc. and thus can be exterminated not in a war but in the right-thinking people detaining or removing the bad ones.

De Benoist's *The Problem of Democracy* subjects the most sacred of all modern pieties, the ideal of liberal mass democracy, to rigorous and unrelenting criticism. The only other contemporary work that I am aware of that offers such a thoroughgoing assault on modern democracy is Hans Hermann Hoppe's *Democracy: The God That Failed*. I gave Hoppe's work an extensive review when it first came out ten years ago. The twentieth century's two leading critics of modern liberal democracy, with its tendencies toward mob rule, were arguably Carl Schmitt and Erik von Kuehnelt-Leddihn. Schmitt attacked liberal democracy from the perspective of a traditional conservative in the mode of Hobbes or Burke, while Kuehnelt-Leddihn offered a critique rooted in a synthesis of Catholic traditionalism and a monarchist variation of classical liberalism reminiscent of Lord Acton.

Hoppe's work is clearly influenced by and somewhat derivative of Kuehnelt-Leddihn, and employs arguments one might expect a conservative Catholic and liberal monarchist to make. De Benoist's observations on democracy more closely resemble and are influenced by those of Schmitt. While Hoppe and Kuehnelt-Leddihn defended classical eighteenth and nineteenth century liberalism against modern egalitarian democracy and its social democratic manifestation, De Benoist like Schmitt before him sees liberalism as the root of the problem. De Benoist offers not classical liberalism but classical democracy as conceived of by the Greeks as the answer to the "problem of democracy" in its modern form. Whereas Hoppe postulates the concept of a society ordered completely on the basis of private property as the alternative to modern democratic institutions, De Benoist offers suggestions that at times resemble the notions of "participatory democracy" or "direct democracy" advanced by certain strands of the Left. These contrasts should make for interesting dialogue and debate on the alternative right.

Guillame Faye's *Why We Fight* differs from much of the literature of the ENR in that while Faye incorporates the essence of the broader New Right philosophy into his analysis, he also demonstrates a greater concern for on-the-ground practical politics, strategic formulations, and particular policy prescriptions in a way that is atypical of ENR thinkers with their general focus on arcane theoretical abstractions, historical interpretations, or "metapolitics." Faye's geopolitical outlook in some ways resembles a melding of the "Eurasianist" idea advanced by Alexander Dugin and the anti-Islamism of Western European Euronationalism. This puts Faye at odds with other strands of the ENR which leans towards at least a tactical solidarity with the Third World and regards Islam as a potential traditionalist ally against globalization and Americanization.

I am inclined to regard Faye's view as appropriate for Europeans and the latter view as more relevant to North Americans. Islam is geographically far removed from North America, and poses no immediate demographic threat. Islamic terrorism directed towards the United States and its allies is for the most part the inevitable "blowback" generated by U.S. foreign policy or, more specifically, the exercise of Zionist influence (whether Jewish or Christian) over American foreign policy in the Middle East. An alliance with Russia against both Americanization and Islamicization may serve the interests of Europeans, but America would be best served by a simple renunciation of globalism and a return to old-fashioned isolationism. Indeed, domestic U.S. Muslims may well be valuable allies against domestic Zionism.

The European New Right clearly has much to offer to ordinary conservatives looking for ideas of infinitely greater substance than what is typically found on talk radio, FOX News, or the subcultures of American right-wing populism. But the philosophy of the ENR might well prove to be the bridge that also helps many disaffected leftists to eventually find their way to the alternative right. The thinkers of the ENR have developed a critique of globalization, imperialism, and Americanization every bit as thorough and radical as that offered by neo-Marxists like Immanuel Wallerstein, indeed even more so. Likewise, the ENR possesses a critique of consumerism, recognition of ecological issues, anticlericalism and critique Christianity that avoids the shrill bigotry of the "new atheists" that at times resembles but is more substantive than that offered by the Left. The ENR emphasis on the sovereignty and self-preservation of all peoples might even appeal to non-white nationalist, separatist, or autonomist movements.

Writers of the ENR have also advanced an intelligent and sincere but measured social and cultural conservatism that lacks the "homosexual-atheist-abortionist-under-every-bed" hysteria of the American right-wing. ENR thought upholds masculine and feminine identities without sinking into crass misogyny, and De Benoist has even controversially called for solidarity with Third World nationalism against US imperialism in a way that resembles a rightist version of Chomsky, and advocated a federated European "empire" of autonomous ethnic, cultural, and national identities that is reminiscent of the Holy Roman Empire (which, as Voltaire said, was neither holy, nor Roman, nor an empire). Meanwhile, the ENR-sympathetic *Telos* journal has postulated a critique of the modern liberal-managerial "new class" that greatly resembles Bakunin's early critique of Marxism.

If we are going to build a rightist opposition in North America that is worthy of the legacy of Nietzsche, Pareto, Schmitt, Mencken, Ortega, and Junger, and is not merely a movement of useful idiots for the neoconservatives, military-industrial complex, and right-wing of the U.S. ruling class as so-called "movement conservatism" often is, then it would appear that the ideas of the European New Right are thus far the best thing going.

# Benoist's Criticisms of the Contemporary Pieties of "Democracy" and "Human Rights"

In his important work *Beyond Human Rights: Defending Freedoms* (Arktos, 2011), Alain De Benoist aptly summarizes the first article of faith of the present day secular theocracy which reigns in the Western world:

> One proof of this is its dogmatic character; it cannot be debated. That is why it seems today as unsuitable, as blasphemous, as scandalous to criticize the ideology of human rights as it was earlier to doubt the existence of God. Like every religion, the discussion of human rights seeks to pass off its dogmas as so absolute that one could not discuss them without being extremely, stupid, dishonest, or wicked...(O)ne implicitly places their opponents beyond the pale of humanity, since one cannot fight someone who speaks in the name of humanity while remaining human oneself.

While reading the above passage, I was instantly reminded of a particularly venal leftist critic who once amusingly described me as "flunking out of the human race" for, among other things, promoting the work of Benoist. The zealous religiosity which the apostles of human rights attach to their cause is particularly ironic given the nebulous and imprecise nature of their cherished dogma. As Thomas Szasz observed:

> Never before in our history have political and popular discourse been so full of rights-talk, as they are today. People appeal to disability rights, civil rights, gay rights, reproduction rights (abortion), the right to choose (also abortion), the right to health care, the right to reject treatment...and so forth, each a rhetorical device to justify one or another social policy and its enforcement by means of the coercive apparatus of the state.

Indeed, contemporary "rights-talk" often resembles the scene in one of the *Star Trek* films where Captain Kirk and his cohorts are engaged in negotiations of some sort with the Klingons and the Chekhov character raises the issue of the Klingons' lack of regard for "democracy and human rights." A Klingon responds by denouncing the term "human rights" as "racist" (presumably because Klingons are excluded from the human rights pantheon).

Benoist traces the development of modern "human rights" ideology and explores how the concept of "rights" has changed throughout history. In the classical world, "rights" were conceived of as being relative to an individual's relationship to a particular community. Someone possessed "rights" because they were a citizen of a specific political entity or some other institutional context. The notion of abstract "rights" in a quasi-metaphysical sense was non-existent. Benoist considers the ideology of human rights to be an outgrowth of Christian universalism. Christianity introduced the concept of an individual soul that is eternal, transcendent, and independent of one's specific social identity. Out of the Christian notion of the transcendent soul emerged the Enlightenment doctrine of "natural rights." These rights are assumed to be universal and immutable.

Yet the very concept of "rights" as conceived of in this manner has itself undergone a number of profound metamorphosis. In its early phase, rights doctrine recognized only the Lockean negative liberties of "life, liberty, and property" and so forth. With the advent of ideologies like socialism or progressive liberalism the rights doctrine began to include what are now called "positive" rights. FDR's famous "four freedoms" are an illustration of the foundations of this perspective. With the racial and cultural revolutions of the postwar era, rights doctrine took on a whole new meaning with "rights" now including exemption from discrimination on the basis of ethnicity, gender, sexual orientation, disability and an increasingly long list of other things. This certainly would have come as a shock to the great apostle of "natural rights," Thomas Jefferson, who, as the Left never ceases to remind us, was a white male slaveholder who thought homosexuals should be castrated.

The definition of "human rights" continues to become increasingly murky over time. Benoist provides an apt illustration of the escalating imprecision of the rights doctrine by citing this quote from Pierre Manent:

> To respect the dignity of another human being is no longer to respect the respect which he conserves in himself for the moral law; it is today, more and more, to respect the choice that he has made, whatever this choice may be, in the realization of his rights.

Benoist describes the predictable outcome of the rights doctrine that is now observable in contemporary politics:

> The present tendency...consists in converting all sorts of demands, desires, or interests into 'rights.' Individuals, in the extreme case, would have the 'right' to see no matter what demand satisfied, for the sole reason that they can formulate them. Today, to claim rights is only a way of seeking to maximize one's interests.

Particularly disastrous has been the fusion of the rights doctrine with mass democracy and the parallel growth exhibited by these two. Hans Hermann Hoppe has observed that a mass democracy comprised of an infinite number of interest groups making infinite rights claims is simply a form of low-intensity civil war. Likewise, Welf Herfurth has demonstrated how the very meaning of "democracy" has changed over time whereby earlier definitions of this concept, even in their modern liberal variations, have been abandoned and "democracy" has simply become a pseudonym for the limitless right to personal hedonism.

A paradoxical effect of the infinite expansion of the rights doctrine has been the simultaneously infinite growth of the state. Fustel de Coulandges described the political order of pre-modern Europe:

> At the top of the hierarchy, the king was surrounded by his great vassals. Each of these vassals was himself surrounded by his own feudatories and he could not pronounce the least judgment without them...The king could neither make a new law, nor modify the existing laws, nor raise a new tax without the consent of the country...If one looks at the institutions of this regime from close quarters, and if one observes their meaning and significance, one will see they were all directed against despotism. However great the diversity that seems to reign in this regime, there is, however, one thing that unites them: this thing is obsession with absolute power. I do not think any regime better succeeded in rendering arbitrary rule impossible.

Benoist contrasts this with subsequent political developments in European civilization:

> The end of the feudal regime marked the beginning of the disintegration of this system under the influence of Roman authoritarianism and the deadly blows of the centralized state. Little by little, hereditary royalty implemented a juridicial-administrative centralization at the expense of intermediary bodies and regional assemblies. While the communal revolution sanctioned the power of the nascent bourgeoisie, the regional parliaments ceased to be equal assemblies and became meetings of royal officers. Having become absolute, the monarchy supported itself upon the bourgeoisie to liquidate the resistances of the nobility.

Indeed, it could be argued that a similar process is presently transpiring whereby the New Class (or what Sam Francis called the "knowledge class" or what Scott Locklin regards as simply a new upper middle class) is aligning itself with the central government for the purpose of destroying the traditional WASP elite and marginalizing the traditional working to middle classes just as the nascent bourgeoisie of earlier times aligned itself with absolute monarchies against the nobility.

The growth of the rights doctrine has of course brought with it the explosive growth of rights-enforcement agencies and bureaucrats as any small business owner or self-employed person who has dealt with Occupational Health and Safety Administration would agree. Likewise, the autonomy of regions, localities, and the private sector has been nearly entirely eradicated in the name of creating rights for an ever expanding army of grievance groups and their advocates. Benoist discusses how the rights doctrine has also resulted in the phenomenal growth of the legal system. Today, there is virtually no aspect of life that is considered to be beyond the reach of state regulation or prohibition. Says Pierre Manent:

> In the future, if one depends principally upon human rights to render justice, the 'manner of judging' will be irreparable. Arbitrariness, that is to say precisely what our regimes wanted to defend themselves against in instituting the authority of constitutionality, will then go on increasing, and will paradoxically become the work of judges. Now, a power which discovers that it can act arbitrarily will not delay in using and abusing this latitude. It tends towards despotism.

Far more dreadful than the use of "rights" as a pretext for enlarging civil bureaucracies and creeping statism in domestic and legal matters has been the application of the "human rights" ideology to international relations. Benoist points out the irony of how the military imperialism that the decolonialization movements were ostensibly supposed to end has been revived under the guise of "humanitarian intervention." The doctrine of "humanitarian intervention" not only contravenes the international law established by the Peace of Westphalia but as well the Charter of the United Nations: "*It suggests that every state, whatever it be, can intervene at will in the internal affairs of another state, whatever it be, under the pretext of preventing 'attacks on human rights.'"* The effect of this doctrine is the simple sanctioning of aggressive war without end.

Plato's observation that a democratic regime on its deathbed is most typically characterized by a combination of individual licentiousness and creeping political tyranny would seem to be apt assessment of our present condition. As one Facebook commentator recently suggested:

Barbarism. Take a picture, we need to get it down for future civilizations. They need to know how the dialectic works: the negation of parental and local authority does NOT lead to freedom, or does so only briefly. That negation is in turn negated by a soft totalitarianism, now becoming harder and more crystallized in order to fill the vacuum of authority. If we record it for them, when some future Neo-Enlightenment philosopher promises liberty and equality circa 2800 CE, he can be properly dressed down before he does any damage.

Hear, hear!

# *Bibliography*

## Julius Evola

Cremo, Michael A. *Human Devolution: A Vedic Alternative to Darwin's Theory*. Torchlight Publishing, 2003.

Evola, Julius. *Eros and the Mysteries of Love: The Metaphysics of Sex*. English translation. New York: Inner Traditions, 1983. Originally published in Italy by Edizioni Meditterranee, 1969.

Evola, Julius. *Revolt Against the Modern World: Politics, Religion, and Social Order in the Kali Yuga*. English translation by Guido Stucco. New York: Inner Traditions, 1995. From the 1969 edition. Originally published in Milan by Hoepli in 1934.

Evola, Julius. *The Yoga of Power: Tantra, Shakti, and the Secret Way*. English translation by Guido Stucci. New York: Inner Traditions, 1992. Originally published in 1949.

Pomeroy, Wardell. *Dr. Kinsey and the Institute for Sex Research*. New York: Harper & Row, 1972.

Sharaf, Myron. *Fury on Earth: A Biography of Wilhelm Reich*. Da Capo Press, 1994.

Wegierski, Mark. The New Right in Europe. *Telos*, Winter93/ Spring 94, Issue 98-99.

# Aleister Crowley

"An Account of A.'.A.'." In *Gems from the Equinox*. St. Paul, MI: Llewellyn, 1974, pp. 31-41.

"An Appeal to the American Republic." In *The Works of Aleister Crowley*. Des Plaines, IL: Yogi, n.d., pp. 136-40.

*Atlantis: The Lost Continent*. Malton, ON, Canada: Dove, n.d.

*The Book of the Law*. York Beach, ME: Weiser, 1976.

"Concerning the Law of Thelema." In *The Equinox*, Vol. III, No. 1, New York: Weiser, 1974, pp. 225-38.

*The Confessions*. London: Arkana - Penguin, 1989.

*The Heart of the Master*. Montreal, PQ: 93 Pub., 1973.

"An Intimation with Reference to the Constitution of the Order." In *The Equinox*, Vol. III, No. 1, pp. 239-46.

"Khabs Am Pekht." In *Gems from the Equinox*, pp. 99-110.

*The Law Is for All*. Phoenix, AZ: Falcon, 1983.

"The Law of Liberty." In *The Equinox*, Vol. III, No. 1, pp. 45-52.

Liber Aleph: *The Book of Wisdom or Folly*. York Beach, ME: Weiser, 1991.

"Liber Porta Lucis." In *Gems from the Equinox*, pp. 651-55.

"Liber Trigrammaton." In *The Law Is for All*, pp. 339-44.

"Liber Tzaddi vel Hamus Hermeticus." In *Gems from the Equinox*, pp. 657-62.

*The Magical Record of the Beast 666.* Montreal, PQ: 93 Pub., 1972.

*Magick in Theory and Practice.* Secaucus, NJ: Castle, 1991.

*Magick without Tears.* Tempe, AZ: Falcon, 1973.

"The Message of the Master Therion." In *The Equinox*, Vol. III, No.1, pp. 39-43.

"An Open Letter to Those Who May Wish to Join the Order." In *The Equinox*, Vol. III, No. 1, pp. 207-24.

*The Scientific Solution of the Problem of Government.* Ordo Templi Orientis, 1936.

*The Secret Rituals of the O.T.O.* Publication information not available.

"Thien Tao." *Konx Om Pax.* Des Plaines, IL: Yogi, n.d., pp. 53-67.

# Corneliu Codreanu

Barbu, Zeev (2003). "Romania: The Iron Guard", in Aristotle A. Kallis (ed.), *The Fascism Reader*. London: Routledge, p.195-201.

Hari, Johan (2009). "Blood, Rage & History: The World's First Terrorists." *The Independent*, October 12, 2009.

Hunter, Jack (2009). "Casualties of Diversity." *Taki's Magazine*, November 15, 2009.

Junger, Ernst (1993). "On Danger." *New German Critique*, No. 59 ( Spring/Summer 1993).

Payne, Stanley G. (1995). *A History of Fascism 1914-1945*. Madison: University of Wisconsin Press, pp. 277-289.

Preston, Keith (2011). "The Nietzschean Prophecies: Two Hundred Years of Nihilism and the Coming Crisis of Western Civilization." *The Radical Tradition: Philosophy, Metapolitics & the Conservative Revolution*, edited by Troy Southgate (Primordial Traditions, 2011).

Preston, Keith (2006). *Propaganda by the Deed, Fourth Generation Warfare and the Decline of the State: An Examination of the History of the Decline of the State's Monopoly on Violence and Warmaking*. Archived at http://attackthesystem.com/propaganda-by-the-deed-fourth-generation-warfare-and-the-decline-of-the-state/

Primo de Rivera, Jose Antonio (1936). "Carta a los militares de Espana." Archived at http://www.rumbos.net/ocja/jaoc0189.html

Van Creveld, Martin (1999). *The Rise and Decline of the State*. Cambridge University Press.

Volovici, Leon (1991). *Nationalist Ideology and Antisemitism: The Case of Romanian Intellectuals in the 1930s*. Oxford: Pergamon Press, 1991.

## Alain De Benoist

Benoist, Alain. *The Problem of Democracy*. London: Arktos, 2011.

Benoist, Alain. *Beyond Human Rights*. London: Arktos, 2011

Faye, Guillaume. *Archeofuturism – European Visions of the Post-Catastrophic Age*. London: Arktos, 2010.

Faye, Guillaume. *Why We Fight: Manifesto of the European Resistance*. London: Arktos, 2011.

Faye, Guillaume. *Convergence of Catastrophes*. London: Arktos, 2012.

O'Meara, Michael. *New Culture, New Right: Anti-Liberalism in Postmodern Europe*, (Second Edition). London: Arktos, 2013.

Hoppe, Hans Hermann. *Democracy: The God That Failed: The Economics and Politics of Monarchy, Democracy and Natural Order.* Piscataway, NJ: Transaction Publishers, 2001.

Kuehnelt-Leddihn, Erik von. *Leftism Revisited: From de Sade and Marx to Hitler and Pol Pot.* Washington, D.C.: Regnery Gateway, 1990

Sunic, Tomislav. *Against Democracy and Equality: The European New Right*, (Third Edition). London: Arktos, 2010.

Sunic, Tomislav. *Homo Americanus: Child of the Postmodern Age.* Charleston: SC: Book Surge Publishing, 2007.

Sunic, Tomislav. *Postmortem Report: Cultural Examinations from Postmodernity - Collected Essays.* Shamley Green, UK: The Paligenesis Project, 2010.